The little Book of Eve

Learning to live in **TRUTH** & **FAVOUR**

SHIRLEY HIGHAM

www.truthandfavour.com

British Library Cataloging in Publication Data
A record of this book is available from the British Library

ISBN 978-1-78808-877-0

Printed and bound in Great Britain

Published by Shirley Higham
www.truthandfavour.com

We acknowledge all those individuals that have made a contribution to
help bring this body of work together, with special thanks to
Becky, Emily, Jo, Karen, Kim, Rachel and Ruth.

Photography by Matthew Higham (MatthewHighamCreative)

Branding, design and self-publishing support by Simplicate
www.simplicate.org

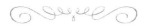

Dedicated to every
'God First Gorgeous Girl'
who courageously dares to
believe the voice of the Father.

CONTENTS

THE JOURNEY

SIGNPOSTS AND STEPPING STONES

THE FINAL DESTINATION

When I consider Your heavens,
the work of Your fingers, the moon
and the stars, which You have
ordained; what is man that
You take thought of him, and the
son of man that You care for him?
Yet You have made him a little
lower than God, And You crown
him with glory and majesty!

Psalm 8: 3-5 (NASB)

Chapter 1

BACK TO THE BEGINNING

Sometimes in life, you have to go back to the beginning. You have to turn your head and cast your eyes back to the very start. You simply have to give your attention again to the foundations and, before you take another stride on the journey, you have to step back and remember where it all began.

I can remember years ago walking in the Lake District with my then 'soon-to-be' husband, Kevin. Now, either I had bullishly insisted or he had foolishly persuaded me to navigate; either way the end result was the same. Pretty soon, we were hopelessly astray, halfway up a mountain, totally off the beaten track with not another living soul in sight except for a few bleating stray sheep. Anxiety was beginning to rise and so were the volume levels of our conversation. However, all was not lost. As we turned around a craggy outcrop, we realised we were stood at the head of a valley. The views were spectacular and all we could do was stand in awe at the breathtaking sight. With the gentle breeze on our faces, we surrendered to the waves of tranquillity and all feelings of irritation melted away. Without hesitation, we sank into the moist earth to rest our increasingly weary bones and sore feet. It was a magical experience, the type you cannot artificially create, a truly rare and precious moment. But when it was time to move on, we had no choice but to go back to the beginning of the walk and try again to navigate to our intended destination. In fact, the only way we could be fully sure of the path we needed to take was to go back to the start and begin again.

If I were to look back across my thirty-plus years as a Christian believer, the sight would be a rich patchwork of textures and colours. There would be amazing moments of brilliant gold and crimsons when I have been fully convinced of God's existence and His immense, passionate love for me. There would also be pale shades of God's peace and kindness, and rolling ripples throughout of blues and greens representing His forgiveness and grace, a blessing that I have so gratefully lived with every day of my life. Layer upon layer of moments in time when the Holy Spirit has brought a revelation of God's love which has wrapped around my heart and soul like a warm, soft blanket. But, if I am honest, there would be something else. Dark threads of doubt and fear that weave sinisterly throughout the tapestry in stark contrast to the rest of the fabric. Doubt that whispers in my ear that God is not real at all and that my faith is simply some psychedelic hoax, there just to support my weak, insecure ego. The fear which cries out, if only God and those around me knew the real me, they would turn their faces from me and I would be alone forever. Countless single strands, of course, a dusky yarn which has at times left me living under a shadow, believing that God is far away and as untouchable as the moon.

But I have been on a journey ... and it all started when I went back to the beginning. And this has not just been 'my' journey. I have had the privilege of walking alongside many courageous, amazing women who have also taken this path. Several of their stories are told throughout the pages of this book.

'Every ending is a new beginning.
Through the grace of God,
we can always start again.'

Marianne Williamson

Chapter 2

A DAY TO REMEMBER

I have to say I honestly believe that, throughout the ages of time, there has been no greater moment in the history of the universe than the day Jesus Christ rose from the dead. The event simply changed everything. It is remarkable that God came to Earth and even more remarkable that He hung on a tree in an act of complete sacrifice to save us from our sin. However, that God did those things from a place of love and compassion towards humanity leaves us humbled, bewildered and astonished.

But then, as if that were not enough, we are faced with the overwhelming event of the resurrection. In this, we discover the evidence for the perfection and the deity of Jesus. The power of the Son of God is displayed and a cataclysmic blow is delivered against the greatest enemies of humanity. Death and Satan are defeated in a single and ultimate act of sacrifice. Paul was so correct, when he wrote in the Book of Corinthians, that if Christ had not been raised from the dead, our faith was 'worthless': such is the magnitude of that day.

However, if we are to fully understand the extent of the work of Jesus and the implications for our Christian walk today, we have to explore much further back. If we simply look back as far as the life and death of Jesus, we will miss something of the reason He had to come at all. We can discover new insights by glancing back in time to when the Earth was new and all things in God's creative imagination were just forming into reality. Insights which help us to understand the lights and darks that contrast our character and make up our ever-changing behaviour and emotions. We can gain a greater understanding into the reason for our shifting doubts and fears. Most importantly, we can begin to comprehend how an innocent man, who hung on a tree over two thousand years ago, could possibly change the very essence of our being, bringing greater vibrancy and colour. But to fully explore these important things, we must be willing to go back to the beginning.

And so, some years ago, I was asked to speak at a Mothering Sunday Service in my home church and I decided to speak about Eve. In many ways, the preaching that day was like any other. I prepared it in the same manner and delivered it like I always did. But somewhere in the process I caught a glimpse of something that captured my imagination. A question rose within me which I had never asked before and, in my quest for the answer, I found myself venturing along a path that would completely change my perspective, and my heart, forever.

You see, the question which caught my attention and became my mission to answer was this: What really happened in the Garden of Eden? Now I suspect that, for many of you, if I were to personally ask you this question, the reply would simply slip straight off the tongue. 'Well, Shirley,' you would reply, 'sin entered the world'. And you would be correct. It is a term we are so familiar with, a phrase we are so used to saying that we skip over the words like skimming stones over still water. After all, I would suspect that most people reading this book would have heard the story told a thousand times of Adam, Eve and the forbidden fruit. However, when 'sin' entered the Garden of Eden, it did not come alone. As I began to explore the early chapters of Genesis, it became more and more obvious that beneath the canopy of 'sin' came a number of other vile creatures such as 'fear' and 'doubt', in truth, the very sentiments I had been struggling with my entire life. 'So', I thought, 'this is where it all began, right here, in the beginning.'

And what of the death of Jesus? Like the skimming stones mentioned previously, we are taught that His death brought freedom, healing and faith. And although I understood the 'fact', I am not sure I understood the process. Whilst I believed His death paid the penalty for my sin on the cross, I had yet to fully realise how His death helped me to put aside the doubt I felt daily or the fear I may face tomorrow. What difference did the death of Jesus really make to all that happened in the very beginning?

And so my quest began. By the grace of God, this little book tells the story of the journey myself and others have walked and the amazing life-changing discoveries we have found.

THE JOURNEY

In the beginning, Lord,
you laid the foundations
of the earth, and the heavens
are the work of Your hands.

Hebrews 1: 10 (NIV)

THE CREATION OF WOMAN

As the Trinity sat in glory and splendour, they considered the wonder of the Earth they had made. It was everything they had hoped it would be. Towering, majestic mountain ranges amid vast, open landscapes, deep oceans teaming with colour and beauty, an immense, extensive array of wildlife, from microscopic organisms to impressive, regal beasts. And all this existed within the intricate processes of life that the Godhead had designed and breathed into them. They had poured all their creativity and love into the making of the world and in their heart, they knew that it was good.

Yet, as they scanned their spectacular world, their eyes fell naturally on Adam. He was by far their most precious creation because it was into Adam that they had emptied so much of themselves. Here was a being made in their very image, designed to reflect their awesome glory and brilliance. It was with Adam in mind that they had made all other things, longing for him to know the joy and pleasure of governing the Earth with them and reigning alongside them for eternity.

And now it was time to create for Adam a partner, since the Godhead knew that it was not good for him to be alone. They placed Adam in a deep, restful sleep and, taking a rib from his side, they formed a new creation. They fashioned her so perfectly, with faultless skill and deepest, tender devotion. She, too, would be made in the image of the Almighty and, together with Adam, would mirror the very likeness of the Triune God. When Adam saw her, his heart was overwhelmed with gratitude because he knew that at last he had a companion with whom he could share his life. He gave her the name 'woman', a term which we now understand to be the name Eve.

(Paraphrased from Genesis 1: 26 - 2: 23)

Chapter 3

THE BEAUTY OF EVE

Over the years, I have heard the name Eve mentioned many times in books and sermons, but in every case, the comments have been less than complimentary: 'Eve was deceived'; 'She brought sin into the world'; 'Eve, the ultimate temptress, enticed her husband to eat the fruit and sin'. Poor Eve, she didn't have the best reputation. But, if you take the time to think about it, before the fall Eve really did have the most extraordinary life. In fact, her encounter with life would have been very different from our own. She lived an existence no woman in history has ever experienced. She lived in a world of total faultlessness and profound beauty.

The Bible tells us that she and Adam were placed in a garden called Eden. The word Eden is close to the Aramaic word which, when translated, means fruitful and well-watered. It is a word which means 'the garden of God' and it conjures up images of paradise. I guess for each of us the term 'paradise' may differ a little. Maybe you picture beautiful open spaces, turquoise seas and golden beaches or perhaps you prefer high mountains or deep forest? For me, paradise is a place of deep lush vegetation with an abundance of wildlife, and within walking distance of a vendor selling great coffee with little portions of chocolate on the side! No matter our interpretation, it is unlikely that our concept of paradise comes anywhere close to Eden. You see, the Bible tells us that God 'placed' Adam and Eve in Eden; it was His choice of dwelling for them and as such, it must have been absolutely perfect.

But it wasn't just the environment of the garden that made Eden paradise.

2015 was a year of unprecedented change in the Higham house. Kevin, my husband, went on staff in our local church, my oldest son got married and my youngest son left home and moved continent! I left a 25-year career as a nurse and, sadly, I lost my best friend and precious older sister, as she went to be with Jesus.

Suddenly, among all this shifting sand, a new favourite phrase appeared in the air. 'Life is too short.' It became a bit of a byword for taking risky decisions and making outrageous choices. But behind the seemingly flippant indifference, there was something more sinister lurking.

In truth, it was a primal fear that somehow we had to squeeze everything in before the end came, to take life and drain every last ounce from it before the 'cliff edge' drew near and it was all over. It was the fear of finality, a concept young Eve would have never encountered. Eve lived in a world where there would have been no concept of time running out or her life coming to an end. There would have been no fear of death, only an impression that each day would beget the next, from sunrise to sunset, continuously tumbling on into eternity. Imagine what it must have been like to literally have had 'all the time in the world'? Unlike Adam, Eve had never known a time when her soulmate had not existed by her side, and she had no reason to believe that things would ever change. She had no knowledge of war, no fear of natural disaster and no concept of disease. All the events we experience, that can bring a sudden or gradual termination to the things we hold as precious and enduring, would have been alien to the first lady of humanity, as different as the clearness of pure water is to the blackness of pitch ink.

Equally, Eve would have never thought of going off to 'find herself'. There would have been no hypothetical gap year to experience the delights of Asia or South America before taking up her place at 'Eden City University'. Eve knew exactly who she was, where she had come from and why she was on Earth. Her virgin mind had never conceived the notion that her race had its origins in a primordial soup, evolving through the species until she became the disordered mixture of DNA called humanity. Without much of the misinformation we are exposed to today, Eve could appreciate the reality of her creation in its purest form. She was conceived in the thoughts of a holy God, fashioned with His imagination from the earth that He had created, into the image that He alone had envisioned. He had purposed her to rule with Adam, and together they would see the Earth filled with men and women who mirrored the glory and wonder of His majesty. For Eve knew from the very beginning that it was His image she had been born to reflect. She would have looked to the future with expectation and hope, quite sure of the world and her place in it.

"

'So hand in hand they passed,
the loveliest pair that ever
since in love's embraces met —
Adam the goodliest man of
men since born his sons; the fairest
of her daughters Eve.'

John Milton, 'Paradise Lost'

Chapter 4

FOR THE LOVE OF EVE

It has to be said that the level of love and companionship Eve would have been exposed to would have been unprecedented. It is simply impossible for us to fully comprehend how it must have felt for Eve to have experienced such an immense richness of love from both God and Adam. Imagine being able to embrace the warmth and affection offered to you from another with the freedom of no inhibitions or hesitations on your part. Goodness! There are times when I have trouble receiving a simple one-dimensional compliment! A person can tell me that my hair looks great and I catch myself wondering if there is an ulterior motive.

But for Eve there would have been no barriers, no suspicions, and no mistrust. She could allow herself to be wholly loved, to be completely awash with the affections of Adam, and to be drenched in the acceptance and love of an almighty God, without the slightest concern or the mildest resistance.

Then consider being able to give that same wholesome, unselfish love in return without any wavering or uncertainty. The level of depth and authenticity in her relationship with both God and Adam must have been stunning. No wonder they were able to live out their days in Eden, before the fall, in nakedness. They really had nothing to hide. There were no unspoken secrets from centuries past between them, no hidden skeletons in the cupboard which may one day tumble out and change everything. Eve was able to love with an open heart and with everything she had because there was nothing stored away in the shadows.

This first lady, who was made in the image of the one whose name is love, was able to show a level of affection so alien to many of us today. Eve was able to love 'herself'.

She walked the Earth in a world where material possessions didn't matter, created before 'the Joneses' had ever bought their first starter home. Eve inhabited a land before television advertisers dictated their visions of success, and airbrushed, size zero models told us the image of 'true beauty'. With no-one to impose the expectations of who Eve should be, except those who loved her perfectly, and with no sinful comparison to distort the image of who she really was, Eve believed herself to be both lovable and beautiful.

For many years sociologists have debated whether our personalities develop more through nature or nurture. So is it the genes we are born with, or the environment we grow up in, that determine the sort of adult we will become? For Eve, the question is practically irrelevant because, regardless of the answer, the outcome would be the same. Created in the image of a holy God whose nature is love, and raised in a perfect garden with purpose and an eternal perspective, Eve would have flourished. She would have been confident and vibrant and full of life. I think she would have been a woman of great contentment and rather simple beauty. In fact, if I am honest, she would have been the kind of woman I have spent most of my life longing to be, which is hardly surprising since Eve was the kind of woman we were always meant to be: the woman that God always intended us to be.

Unfortunately, however, the perfection of Eden was about to be shattered by a drama in which Eve would play a leading role. The soft, sweet nature of fruitfulness and water, exchanged for the sting of hard ground, thorns and thistles. Carefree innocence and nakedness of nurture exchanged for coverings and protection. And the beauty of Eve would never be seen again in her lifetime.

THE DEVIL'S RUSE

Now the snake was the most stealthy and cunning of all of Eden's creatures, which made him the perfect choice. The devil knew that he could use the serpent's smooth voice to gently and covertly manipulate Eve. If the strategy worked, then God would be forced to watch His entire, precious creation suffer, which of course was the whole purpose of the plan.

He waited for Eve near her favourite tree and watched her as she meandered through the orchard towards him. With great control and measure, he presented her with a new and seemingly innocent view of God's words. Slowly, he encouraged her to question God's truth and probe into His intentions. 'Think again Eve, did God really say that? What is God trying to keep from you? Would you not also like to be as God?' The devil understood this particular desire only too well and it was easy for him to articulate it. As he gently wooed her, he watched with tantalising relish as she raised the forbidden fruit to her lips. In that second, his soul almost exploded within him. This, he knew, would be like a dagger to the heart of God and he savoured every second.

As he slid away, he smiled to himself. At last, she preferred him to God. At last, she chose to sit under his authority. At last, he was in the place he always knew he should be, above God. His opinion higher, his voice higher, his desire higher. Nothing in all creation could explain the satisfaction he felt at that moment. He had snatched from the Almighty's hands everything God held as beloved and it tasted simply delicious.

(Paraphrased from Genesis 3: 1-6a)

Then you will know the truth,
and the truth will set you free.

JO'S STORY

I would love to tell you a bit about my journey, of how I believed a lie, how that affected me, and the changes that happened once the truth came.

Writing this down on paper, it sounds almost unbelievable now, but this was my reality. I believed the lie that I was insignificant. I considered others more important than myself and I considered my opinions, ideas and wishes as secondary. The outworking of this lie made me unable to accept any praise when I did anything well, or to believe the truth of who my Father in Heaven said I was without thoughts that I was being proud.

The turnaround to me recognising truth takes me back to a time when I met with some trusted friends. We were praying for one another and encouraging one another to go for 'our dreams'. I told them my goal of the year was to know in my heart (not just in my head) that I am royalty, that I am a loved princess of Jesus, the King of Kings.

I had read a book all about this subject and had come across something called 'false humility'. As I read about this disabling thing, it was like I was reading about myself, my life and my thoughts. It felt like a thunderbolt had arrested my heart and as I read, I knew it was me. False humility was described as something that stopped people from realising their true potential, from knowing the truth of who they are. It stopped them from ever being able to accept praise, as they think it is pride. After all, any praise should only be directed to Jesus, right? Now, that bit does sound right - giving praise to Jesus -

but stay with me as I explain more in a moment.

Father God was described as an artist, painting a beautiful picture, a very intricate one with many colours and details. This picture was you and me. Well here was I, pulling down the Father's designed and planned creation, His creative design - ME! I had been unable to give Him praise for making me good at things, my gifts and talents; I hadn't given Him thanks for His design in how He made me. Whenever I had been told 'well done' for something, I immediately didn't accept the praise and said things like, 'Yes Jesus is amazing', 'No, it wasn't me!', or I buried my head in utter embarrassment.

As I finished the chapter, I knew this was something I had to turn away from and say sorry to Jesus for believing. I simply prayed right there and then. There were no lightning strikes or audible voices but, at that exact moment, something had changed, something new had a place in my heart.

From that point on, I can honestly say I was different. I started to believe the truth that I was significant. My favourite phrase to describe this is 'I am significant because He is everything'.

The outworking of this is that I am now able to accept praise from others when I do things well (without feeling in any way big-headed or boastful). And I can tell others when I have done well, rather than focusing on my faults, where I got things wrong or any failures. I am able to take more risks, as I am now more secure in who I am. Friends have seen a massive change in me too, which is exciting since this can only encourage others to believe truth too.

I can accept praise, then privately thank Father for how He made me to be me, for the gifts and talents I have been given; this is not big-headed, it's actually believing the truth!

25

I know now that I have a voice, an opinion to be heard and that I am significant. My husband is awesome, what an encourager. For my birthday, he commissioned an incredible artist to paint a picture of a lioness for me, to remind me of who I now am, a fearless lioness with a significant roar.

Chapter 5

THE DECEPTION
OF EVE

As I took the time to look below the surface, I began to see the start of the events that took Eve down a path she never thought possible. The devil played his part perfectly and Eve was forever changed. If only she had recognised his intentions; if only she had seen the situation for what it really was; if only she had discerned the deception. Poor Eve, if only she had identified that, through the devil's silky words, there lay a detestable and devastating lie.

That day in the garden, the devil approached Eve and he lied to her. He spoke to Eve in the form of a serpent, telling her that she would not die and cunningly questioning her image of her heavenly Father God. He began damaging her faith in the things God had said and presented her with an option that God's motives included withholding something that Eve would benefit from. Suddenly Eve thought she saw things more clearly and it seemed obvious to her what she must do, when all the time, what was really happening was that her eyes were being diverted from the truth, and she was caught up in a deception that would ultimately impact not only her life, but the rest of humanity.

What I had never realised before was that the devil has the sinister ability to take a distorted, hateful lie and make it appear like a perfectly rational thought. It's a skill that he began using in the Garden of Eden and he has been practising the talent across the aeons of time ever since, refining and sharpening and perfecting. He is a master craftsman at deceit and deception, a principle artist in the skill of sedition. I don't know why I never saw it before; after all, the Bible calls the devil the father of lies. This is the devil's chief tactic, to use his words to manipulate humanity into believing something that just isn't true.

And so, with the only weapon the devil had at his disposal, his voice, he softly and deviously uttered his vile suggestions into Eve's ear and, without her even realising it, he blatantly lied to her. He used a creature of great beauty so that Eve would not recognise the darkness behind the masquerade. He twisted words that she would have been familiar with so as to not to confuse her or cause her to investigate too closely the things he was saying. And he did it all with her trusted soulmate, Adam, stood by her side.

And in a second, the world was altered forever.

Chapter 6

TRUTH AND LIES

I remember the day I really began to believe in my heart that I had been lied to. It was a Sunday morning and I was on a Q&A panel in church. Members of the congregation were able to text in any question they chose relating to the Christian faith and the panel would give a response. I have to say, it's one of those 'it seemed like a good idea at the time' moments. You know, when I was asked, I was sure it would be fine, but now sat on the platform, not knowing what questions were being texted my way, I was not so sure. One text read, 'Can a Christian be demonised?'. I don't recall everything I replied but I do remember saying that the most common form of demonisation a person encounters is listening to the voice of the devil and allowing him to influence our thoughts. At that point, I felt something shift. A revelation had occurred and I suddenly knew something in my 'knower' that I had only previously alluded to; I had spent my whole life being deceived.

Lies come in many guises, although their source is always the same. I remember some years ago, when my husband had been asked to work abroad by his employers. He would leave the house early Monday morning and return late evening every other Friday. At the time, our oldest son, Timothy, was three and I noticed that, as the weeks went by, he was becoming quiet and withdrawn. I assumed he was simply missing his daddy and sought to comfort him accordingly. One Friday afternoon, after an excited conversation explaining that when he woke the next morning daddy would be home, I overheard him say something to his trusted teddy bear that shook me to the core. 'If we are good this time, daddy will not go away again.'

I was totally stunned! Immediately in my mind, I began retracing conversations I had had previously with him. Had I ever implied it was due to his behaviour that his dad had to work away? Absolutely not! This was a conclusion Tim had apparently reached all on his own. Sometimes, lies are conclusions we come to that are simply not true. It's as if a whispered suggestion is made and we cannot resist taking it on board. Often, it feels like blaming ourselves is the easiest solution, a way of having just a little piece of control, and so we believe that a situation is our fault even when it isn't. We adopt a lie, a falsehood and we call it our own. Lies can be spoken into our lives by those we know and trust, sometimes with bad intentions to wound and scold us, other times with misplaced good intentions.

You see, the devil's job has been made easier by the fact that we have all grown up in a world of lies. From a very young age, we are told there is a Santa Claus, a Tooth Fairy and even an Easter Bunny. I was told that I was born under a gooseberry bush, but that the caterpillars had eaten their way through the leaves, allowing the rain to turn my hair rusty and that is why I was born with ginger hair! I'm not saying we shouldn't tell fairy tales to our children; they can fuel imagination and often bring great joy. I told my boys that if they played with their belly buttons, their bums would fall off! Some lies appear innocent in nature and it quickly becomes obvious that they are not true.

Wider afield, the advertising industries, while objecting to an obvious lie, have little opposition to a more subliminal message. Adverts tell us we must wear a certain perfume to be beautiful and wanted, or own particular items to be successful, intelligent or popular. Digitally-manipulated models, political spin and industrial misrepresentation have left us surrounded by so much myth and fabrication that we have almost become blind to it. We are sleepwalking through a forest of reality, where we no longer perceive the artificial trees of lies and untruths.

Chapter 7

FERTILE SOIL

The bizarre thing is that we now live in a world where lies are acceptable and truth is treated with suspicion and rejection. Try telling someone that your view about a moral issue or an ethical situation is more valid or more truthful than theirs and see how they respond. Anybody who dares to claim they have 'more' truth, or believe in a 'greater' truth, is rejected as arrogant at best or a dangerous extremist at worst.

Truth has become a little like beauty; it's all about perception. I know I am very blessed because my husband thinks I am beautiful all the time. So when I have my most stunning outfit on and it's one of those occasions when my makeup and hair actually do what I want them to, then he thinks I look beautiful. And when I've just fallen out of bed, wearing the same unattractive pyjamas I've had on for a fortnight and my hair resembles that of the dog then, amazingly, he still thinks I look beautiful.

Today, truth is like beauty; the truth is in the eye of the beholder. It's all about individual perception.

In this fertile soil, the devil has been left to fill our minds with lies which become locked into our subconscious. While some lies appear superficial and innocent, others are dangerous and corrosive. These lies often become difficult to refute. Various lies stay with us our whole lives and they can twist our view of God, ourselves and the world. Some lies simply seem to get a hold of us. They get under our skins, impregnate our thought patterns, impact the everyday decisions we make and can ultimately be incredibly destructive. Many of us will have experienced being called ugly, stupid or useless by a parent, an employer or a teacher at school. Maybe a friend made a throwaway comment one day and suddenly, there it is, attached to the synaptic pathways of your brain, playing over and over again like a broken record, until you cannot function in any other way but in line with the lie.

Without the input of our loving heavenly Father God, this credulous perspective would remain like a permanent imprint on our unsuspecting minds. We would be destined to live out our existence without any concept of truthful reality. However, we are children of a God of love and power and, as such, we always have hope. It is this confidence that is the essence of our Christian walk; this optimism that brings joy and certainty.

Chapter 8

THE WHISPERS
WE LISTEN TO

I n the beauty of the Garden of Eden, among
God's splendid creation, the lies of the devil entered
the world. His motives were to draw God's handiwork
away from the maker, to wound God as deeply as it
is possible to wound any parent by turning their children
against them. Just as with Eve, every lie the devil
has ever told us exists purely to keep us from the truth
of who God really is, so that we will withdraw our love
from Him and despise Him. The devil will say anything
to undermine our understanding of God's divine nature,
His passionate love for us and His endless desire to be in a
relationship with us. But more than any of these, the devil
will do anything and say anything to trick us into believing
that God is not good. If he can do that, he knows that
he will be pulling the linchpin of our trust and everything

else will come crashing down like the proverbial pack of cards.

In the Book of John, the Bible tells us that the devil's job description is to kill and destroy, and he has committed his entire existence to it. By lying to Eve that fateful day, he set about a chain of events that he hoped would make sure God's beautiful creations could never again be all God purposed them to be. His aim was to destroy all that God had said was good and to cause us to function in a way that was a mere shadow of the image God held in His mind when He created us. The devil's plan was to simply stand back and gloat as God was forced to watch humanity settle for tiny, insignificant existences, mere ghosts of their potential selves. And if he could generate a great darkness within us and shatter any resemblance of God's light, then all the better. You see, there is no greater pain for a loving parent than to watch their children destroyed, and there is no deeper agony for a creator than to see their design devastated.

And so the devil continues to lie to us, seeking to undermine our confidence, cause our heads to droop and our hearts to lose all hope. He tells us we are too weak to attempt great things, too insignificant to make a difference, too disgusting to be loved by a holy God or even another human being. He tells us we are too great to need help, too conflicted to ever know peace and too wretched to be worthy of receiving a righteous inheritance. He sits on our shoulder, day after day, and whispers in our ear copious lies that contradict the truths of who God is and who God has made us to be. The devil speaks to us of our failures as a woman, as a wife, as a mother; he suggests that we will never succeed in love or friendship and that we will always be captive to certain habits or sickness or disappointment. Lies. Lies. Lies.

But God had a plan. God always had a plan. He was not taken by surprise and He was not left traumatised or impotent in the wake of the devil's tactics. God knew the devil's heart and was fully aware of what he was capable of. What is more, God loved humanity with a depth no created being could ever fathom. God would do anything, simply anything, to restore His creation to Himself. It is this profound, intense bond of love that the devil simply could not comprehend. Just like any devoted parent, God was prepared to sacrifice Himself, even to death, just to have the opportunity to walk with His children again in the cool of the evening, as He did in Eden. He would suffer great agony if it meant restoring His creation to their former beauty. The devil may have brought lies into the Garden with the purpose of destruction, but the nature of God is restoration and the plan of God would turn even this apparently despairing situation around for humanity's good, and His own supreme glory.

The Word became flesh
and made His dwelling among us.
We have seen His glory,
the glory of the one and only
Son, who came from the Father,
full of grace and truth.

John 1: 14 (NIV)

Chapter 9

ETERNAL GOD
OF TRUTH

God's desire for us is that we are fully restored to all He created us to be. In the depth of His heart, He longs for us to walk again with Him in the fullness of intimate connection and warmth with no hesitation and no restraints. We were never meant to be shackled to lies and falsehoods which diminish our understanding of God and disconnect us from our destinies. We were meant to fly beneath the canopy of God's love and flourish within the frontier of His truth.

And so, etched throughout the pages of the Bible, God's strategy for mankind is revealed. God, who exists outside all known dimensions, had formulated the plan before the beginning of time. You see, when God stands and glimpses across His infinite corridor of time and space, the prized treasure He perceives is us, His precious created humanity. Our first steps towards our freedom from an existence saturated in lies and deception, and into a world of light and truth, is to elevate our heads and do the same. God tenderly longs for us to stop amid the chaos of our lives. Then He gently invites us to cast our eyes across our finite corridor of time and space, and to recognise the prize before us. He calls us to seek Him out, to gaze into His eyes of warmth and love, and to realise that the prize we perceive is none other than God Himself.

You see, the greatest mistake Eve ever made was that she did not recognise the lie the devil told her, and the greatest mistake we will ever make is that we fail to recognise the truth that God has revealed.

In the Gospel of John, Jesus makes an astonishing claim. He announces that He is 'the way and the truth and the life'. In the same way that love is an essential element of God's character, truth is a fundamental part of who Jesus is. It's not merely that He speaks the truth or that He brings truth; Jesus, by His nature, 'is' truth. It is part of the fabric of His very being. He can no more deceive us than God can be unkind to us; He can no more lie to us than God can show us wickedness. Jesus is truth. He is completely honest, totally trustworthy and entirely genuine. When Jesus walked the face of the Earth, He was followed by the multitudes, who would assemble for hours, enthralled by His words of grace and wisdom. He was not known for manipulation or exaggeration, rather he was known for bringing words of enlightenment which opened the eyes of those who were blinded and unseeing. With every breath, Jesus was a carrier of certainty and truth in an age marked by hypocrisy and lies. And this Jesus Christ remains the same yesterday, today and forever. On this fact, the Bible is without hesitation - that Jesus the Son is the exact representation of God the Father. There is no facet of His nature which was perceived on Earth which does not reveal something of the fullness of the Godhead in Heaven. That being the case, it is safe to say that Father God is also 'truth' and can be totally relied upon to never lie to us or lead us astray.

Finally, we are told in the Gospel of John that the third person of the Holy Ghost is also the 'Spirit of truth ... He will guide you into all the truth'. His role is not only to be a personification of truth but to ensure that truth is told and that we are schooled in it. Our loving, heavenly Father has not left us floundering alone in the dark. The Godhead is everything we will ever require to clear our mind of lies and walk again in truth. Against the lies of the devil there is a compendium of accuracy, certainty and fact; against the poison of the devil's lies there is an antidote, the balm of truth. God is the essence of truth and all truth radiates from Him. He is the gateway to which a person may walk and discover an existence free from lies and falsehood.

Our response is to recognise the value of the One who stands before us and to acknowledge that our deliverance is found in Him alone. God offers Himself to us willingly as the perpetual fountain of absolute truth. He takes great joy when we return frequently, enthusiastically, again and again, to bathe in waters which are wholesome and pure, washing away the filth of the devil's falsehoods and quenching our thirst in the sweetest of waters.

"

'You may believe you are responsible for what you do, but not for what you think. The truth is that you are responsible for what you think, because it is only at this level that you can exercise choice.'

Marianne Williamson

Chapter 10

OUT OF THE
DARKNESS

On the 29th of April 1990, I awoke in a state of great anticipation. It was going to be a very special day because I was about to become Mrs Shirley Higham. Months of planning and preparation had preceded the event with every conceivable eventuality considered. Ready to embrace all the excitement the day held and with a spring in my step, I wandered blissfully into the bathroom. Imagine the trauma I experienced when I looked in the mirror and saw an enormous spot reflecting back at me. I was quite sure it wasn't there the night before! But somehow, during my hours of slumber, it had appeared on the end of my nose, all shiny and bright and ready for my husband-to-be, every wedding guest and several dozen snapping, amateur photographers to focus on. My entire body reacted; my eyes filled with tears, my knees weakened and my heart missed several beats. This was one possibility that, in all the chaos of planning, hadn't even crossed my mind. Pretty soon I found myself feeling incensed. How dare this eruption invade my face on this profoundly important day! I started pointing my finger at it, renouncing it, in the name of everyone and everything I could think of - well, I was desperate - and telling it that it 'simply had no right to be there!'. Yet somehow, a few hours later, I was walking down the aisle with confidence, in a flowing ivory gown, a well-placed veil and enough perfectly-pigmented foundation to save the day.

Like any blemish found on the outside, we must resolve and acknowledge that there are thoughts within our minds that simply have no entitlement to be there. Unwelcome, illegitimate untruths that have no place in the mind of a person who professes to belong to God. Statements and phrases that contradict the truth of who God is and who He created us to be. As such, these words are lies and they have their source in the devil, who is the father of lies. We, however, are children of God, the holder of all truth, and therefore lies have no place in our domain.

You see, many years ago I had committed my life to Christ. I had converted to Christianity and asked Jesus to allow each decision I made to reflect the choices He would make for me, from the smallest concerns to the largest issues. I wanted to do things God's way. However, in those early days, I am not sure I had considered including 'my thoughts'. Thoughts, after all, lived firmly in the private arena. I have been raised to believe that no-one had the right to impose on me the views I should hold or the conclusions I should reach. In this part of my world at least, I remained my own master. But one day, whilst reading the Bible, I realised that Jesus had told the people that adultery was already committed once it had entered a person's thoughts. Sinfulness, it would appear, did not only refer to the actions done, but also the thoughts that went through my mind.

Chapter 11

COURAGEOUS CONFESSION

The most devastating lie I ever believed was that I was unlovable. I can trace the root of this lie back to sepia memories of my childhood. Unpleasant recollections of hours spent stood alone in grey, tarmacked, school playgrounds. Decades of feeling 'unacceptable' by those I so desperately wanted to belong to. Years of feeling as if I was in a vacuum, invisible to those I loved, while family fights and arguments battled on around me. By the time I had reached adulthood, I realised I had become an expert at walking into a room full of people, chit-chatting to everyone and connecting with no-one, and that once I had given my superficial greeting, every fibre of my being pulled me towards the exit, aching anxiously to detach myself from the situation. I struggled desperately to believe that anyone would ever really want to spend any time with me. I told myself the lie that the only reason people ever chose to be with me was because I had a skill or talent they wanted to access, and that any thought of friendship or companionship was not on their agenda. I even found myself sat in the company of friends and colleagues, feeling and reacting like they were my enemies, with no justification for my emotions at all.

And so, alone one day, in my lounge, I acknowledged and confessed my sin before God. I stood up and dared to announce that I had believed the lie that I was unlovable. It produced a barrage of emotions. On one hand, there was relief and I burst into tears, overwhelmed by the sadness of the lie, and in-between the sobs, I was laughing at how ridiculous it sounded now that it was out in the open. But even as I calmed myself down, I felt a slight dimension shift. Dragging a lie out into the open had somehow begun to reduce its power and loosen its grasp.

The Bible tells us to 'confess your sins to each other', and it was about this time that I was due to meet with other women who made up the women's ministry team in church. In fragility and honesty, we each presented a lie we had believed to the group. It was a night of gasps of astonishment, of trying to perceive a comprehensible sentence through tears and sobs and unbelievable vulnerability. By the end of the evening, we were all exhausted, but we had also struck a huge blow to the lies that had held us captive.

Jesus knows us intimately and He recognises the achievement and personal growth that can materialise when we are honest, vulnerable and authentic with a trusted group of friends. For in the world of lies, silence and secrecy is king but in the domain of truth, openness and vulnerability reign supreme.

God invites us to navigate the initial steps, along this carefully-prepared path into truth, by acknowledging our closely-held lies and confessing our privately-believed secrets - those thoughts we have entertained that we simply should never have considered true in the first place. He is not distant during this journey, rather He places Himself faithfully by our side. Walking the path with us, He is mimicking each stride we take, eager to guide every step lest our feet should stumble, placing His fingers beneath our forearm ready to uphold us in case we slip and only too willing to grasp our hand should our hearts grow fearful or faint. He is willing us to be brave, to take courage, because He knows that, in the acknowledging and confessing of the habitual lies that we have stoically retained, we will ultimately be a step closer to the person He created us to be. God longs for us to rest on Him as we pursue truth and wholeness because He holds within His mind the image of who we truly are; the picture of our beautiful, untarnished selves. For God is perfectly aware that transformation comes through the renewing of the mind. And He gives all the support and guidance we could ever need without the slightest hint of criticism or the mildest suggestion of condemnation. Like a parent teaching a child to take their first precious steps, our heavenly Father watches us, protective of our every shift and passionate that we do well, such is His unbridled love for us.

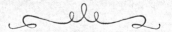

For You created my inmost being;

You knit me together in my

mother's womb. I praise You because

I am fearfully and wonderfully made;

Your works are wonderful, I know

that full well. My frame was not

hidden from You when I was made

in the secret place, when I was woven

together in the depths of the earth.

Your eyes saw my unformed body;
all the days ordained for me were written
in Your book before one of them came
to be. How precious to me are Your
thoughts, God! How vast is the sum of
them! Were I to count them, they would
outnumber the grains of sand – when
I awake, I am still with You.

Psalm 139: 13-18 (NIV)

RUTH'S STORY

I hadn't really thought about it, but even the day before, a friend had prophesied into my life and I had discounted what she had said. It just sounded way too big for me. But as I read through the list of truths with the group of women I was with, God put His finger on one. As I read 'I have amazing potential', it dawned on me I just didn't believe it. I was believing the lie that I didn't have much potential and that my contribution was not worth that much.

Maybe I did believe I had potential once, but somewhere along the way that sense that God could do amazing things through me had faded. Whilst I understood it and agreed with it in practice, I didn't believe it for me. I didn't think my contribution would ever be worth that much. I looked at other women and said to myself, 'they are so amazing', or, 'I could never do that'. I realised that I looked at ministries, opportunities and even maybe some of the things in my heart and said to myself, 'I could never do them. I'm not that sort of woman'.

As I read the truth again, I saw I had put a limit on God using me, on 'how' He could use me and even in His ability to increase my capacity if He needed to. It is so amazing that, in recognising a lie, it loses so much power immediately. I started to believe that in God I do have amazing potential. God's Word says He can do immeasurably more than we can ask or imagine, according to His power that is at work within us; and that includes me. I have the potential to do amazing things in Him.

I don't think I'm there yet, but I am starting to believe Father and step out more. As opportunities have come my way, I have started saying yes, even when they feel a bit (or considerably) beyond what I think I can do. God has always come through. He has used me to speak into people's lives and share His heart for them. I have also loved serving alongside and sharing with other women who are amazing and seeing how each contribution - including mine - is of value and adds something. It has been awesome. I am now excited to see where God will take me as I reach out and choose to see the potential for Him to use me in each opportunity.

Chapter 12

EVE'S PRIVILEGED ACCESS

I love modern technology. Well, let me clarify that statement. I love certain aspects of modern technology. For example, I love being able to stream music. It's great to pay my monthly subscription, select and download any music I choose, store them in little 'playlists' usually titled according to style or mood, and then simply retrieve it by asking my smartphone to begin playing my selected track. How simple can it be? I also love a certain well known search engine. I can merely type in a few choice words about any subject and a wealth of information is instantly available at my fingertips. Ironic really because my husband frequently reminds me of a conversation we had twenty years ago when I naively asked him why anybody would want to access a thing called a 'world wide web'!

However, of all the advances the technological world has afforded us, the thing I most adore is that we now have the ability to communicate with the ones we love with ease and clarity. I can remember, as a young woman away from home for the first time, relying on a public phone box to call home once a week and a few scattered letters were the only means of staying in touch with family and friends. How different the experience has been for my own children. Social media, instant messages and face-to-face calls have meant there has been a constant and immediate line of open contact across the miles. As a mum, of course, I have loved being able to have real-time updates on important events. It's great to have access to that constant, ongoing dialogue of an ever-changing landscape of family circumstances and opinions.

And then there are those wonderful little bubbles that appear on my smartphone screen to let me know a reply to my text is imminent! It means that I am about to find out what the other person is going to reply to my question, statement or request. I am soon to be exposed to their views, thoughts and opinions. My sense of expectation rises, my brain releases a little squirt of dopamine and all is well with the world.

After all, their views and words are terribly important to me; their comments and thoughts are precious ...

... and in the same vein, the Book of Psalms tells us that the thoughts of God towards us are both vast and precious. He is not a distant God who keeps His thoughts and opinions to Himself, rather He opens His heart to us, drawing us into His immense perspective and exposing us to His deepest contemplations.

Before Eve's fateful encounter with the devil, she enjoyed unprecedented access to God as they walked together in the cool of the evening in the Garden. The rhythmic pattern of a daily audience with the almighty God must have been life-giving. Open, unguarded conversations, where details of the day's events were shared in the context of a loving, trustworthy friendship, must have made for the sweetest of meetings. Most importantly, Eve would have perceived the heart and thoughts of God, unhindered in all their beauty and richness. She would have caught a glimpse of His great warmth towards her and understood that she was the apple of His eye. Eve would have basked in His absolute acceptance of her, His beautiful creation. There would have been no lies to contradict His love and no reason to doubt His compassion towards her.

God invites us to be acquainted with His thoughts and His perceptions again, never to dismiss them as unlikely or reject them as untrue, but to elevate them to a place of great worth and importance. As we do this, our minds will be renewed and our hearts will be transformed. In exchange for toxic and treacherous lies, there will be the wholesome and sincere truths of the God of all truth who loves us, without restrictions, and longs for our very best without restraints. He encourages us to live again beneath the canopy of His holy integrity, within the shadow of His goodness and with the embrace of His unconditional love.

"

'God has infinite attention, infinite leisure to spare for each one of us. He doesn't have to take us in the line. You're as much alone with Him as if you were the only thing He'd ever created.'

C. S. Lewis

Chapter 13

GOD'S GRAND LIBRARY

My youngest son, Matthew, once told me he had a vision. He saw himself standing in an ancient library. The tall shelves were made of solid wood and stretched as far as the eye could see. Multiple rows of various volumes neatly placed to access and peruse. He asked God what type of library it was; what knowledge the books contained? To His wonder, God replied that within the pages of each book were every recorded thought that God had ever had about Matthew. They were God's record of everything He believed about him, knew about him and understood about him.

And so it is for you. The thoughts of God towards you have been gathering in the mind of God since the dawn of time. Even before the creation process, God drew together strands of inspiration, ingenuity and creativity and an impression was formed of the beloved child that He would tenderly create. He considered every intricate, slender detail of your being. Like a master craftsman, He left no facet unaccounted for; there is no factor of emotion, no element of appearance and no feature of personality which was not planned with particular care. He allowed His imagination the liberty and freedom to explore who this person may become, what you may achieve and how you may one day love. In due time, He carefully began the breathtaking and complex task of knitting you together in your mother's womb. Measuring the length of each fibre of your being and counting the hairs on your head, this sophisticated and elaborate procedure was completed with perfect precision. And once you were formed, the thoughts of God continued.

There is never a moment that goes by when God is not thinking of us, considering us, musing over our beauty and value. How do I know this? I know this because I have a small insight into how my own thoughts always seem to wander again and again to the ones I truly love. When we love someone, this is how we act; we think about them. We brood, mull and wonder about them multitudes of times each day. Our thoughts collect and gather, and without restraint we find ourselves thinking about them. We recall memories of times spent in each other's presence, we question what occupies their hours and we plan how they may respond at our next encounter. God, who is the ultimate personification of love, can do no other than to think about us because that is the mind of one who loves.

So as the years go by, the thoughts of God gather. He wonders about our days, deliberates about our future, contemplates our hopes and fears. He is interested in our desires, ponders our choices and reflects on our decisions. With the clarity of vision, God sees beyond the façade and pretence that we present to the world. He sees past the barriers and walls, built for our protection and concealment, to the person we truly are. He can see every option open to us, every pathway we may choose to walk down, and each direction our lives may go. He is aware of our favourite colour, who our preferred musicians will be and which flavoured cheesecake we will pick.

In the infinite heart and mind of God, there is simply always more time to think about us and to dwell on every aspect of our lives. And so, as time moves forward, the thoughts of God grow into a compendium of all that He has seen and known about us, into an enormous library of His sacred, precious and wonderful thoughts.

Chapter 14

THE CHALLENGE

S o as I have already written, I recognise completely that God's thoughts concerning us are vast. However, I do find myself facing a personal challenge and it is this. I am constantly asking myself the questions, 'Do I actually believe that the thoughts of God towards me are precious?', 'Do I embrace them as if they have great value?', and, 'Do I perceive them as if they hold immense worth?'.

This is not just about my inner conscious calling me to listen to Him more often, through meditating on His words in the Bible, nor is it the draw of God's Holy Spirt to stop a while and spend time in silence, listening for His still small voice. This question confronts a fundamental aspect of my belief about the relevance of God in my life. Do I hold the words of God with great significance and esteem or am I likely to judge them with low regard? Do I allow them to linger in my mind or am I quick to reject them?

Do I consider them to be precious or am I apt to dismiss them as irrelevant or even, dare I write it, untrue?

You see, it is not enough that we recognise the lies of the devil and refute them. It is not sufficient that we acknowledge and banish the words which linger in our minds, reducing our concept of God's goodness and diminishing us to less than God made us to be. We must also be able to fill the void they leave behind with the beautiful and sacred truths of the thoughts of God; those words which explode our minds with the wonders of His virtues and still our hearts with the tenderness of His acceptance.

The thoughts of God are surely one of the most precious and important things we will ever be privileged to know, bearing in mind that God alone is the champion of all truth and the visionary of an unspoilt humanity. His words about Himself, us and others are totally true and utterly trustworthy. The words of God are the essence of all we need to truly exist as the people God created us to be. But we have to recognise them as precious and we have to believe them to be true. It is this element of acceptance and confidence in the thoughts of God that furnish them with the capacity to alter our reasoning, shift our perception and revolutionise our hearts and minds. It is as we begin to dare to believe that the devil's words are worthless lies and God's are priceless certainties, that we will begin to experience freedom.

God longs for us to believe Him when He tells us that He loves us, that we are His treasured possession, His selected, chosen child, beautiful and significant in His sight. He is passionate that we live our lives reflecting the truths of freedom, peace and joy. God knows our true potential, who we can be when we are unbridled and unhindered by the lies we have spent our lives weighed down and shackled by. He beckons us to listen to His words of truth and to believe the voice of the Almighty, who says that we have potential, that He has plans for our life and that we can do all things through Christ who simply adores us.

Submit yourselves, then, to God.
Resist the devil, and
he will flee from you.

James 4: 7 (NIV)

Chapter 15

THE POWER OF THE SPOKEN WORD

In the Book of Romans we are told that 'faith comes through hearing and hearing through the Word of God'. There is something about being perceptive to the Word of God that fosters faith and cultivates belief in our very souls; the rhythmic motion of repetitive listening to the thoughts of God as recorded in the Bible, and then proclaiming them. This action deepens our level of belief in truth and assists us to walk in a greater measure of faith, redefining and solidifying our identity, destiny and relationship with Father God. It is through this medium that the voice of the one whose desire is to torment and diminish us is dampened and, finally, we are free to hear the voice of the one who loves and cherishes us.

This discovery has had an enormous influence on our church community. As a body of Christian believers, we have challenged one another to seek out someone we trust, a person we feel safe and secure with, and then, after confessing aloud the lies we believe, to verbally proclaim God's truth so that we may hear it.

On one occasion, we purchased small, heart-shaped mirrors and handed them to each of the women attending our regular women's event. On the glass, we had scribed the word 'beautiful'. During the course of the evening, we encouraged each person present to look deep within their own eyes and declare the truth about themselves that, regardless of the opinions of the world, in the sight of God they were beautiful. For many women, this task proved more difficult than expected. A few confident individuals were able to make the proclamation without hesitation. Some women sat in silence, unable to even look themselves in the eye, their self-worth so diminished. However, there were those who attended that night who would say they will never be the same again. Speaking God's truth over themselves, giving permission to see themselves as God saw them, simply changed everything.

Proverbs informs us that 'life and death are in the power of the tongue'; that in itself is a phenomenal statement! However, if we are crafted in the image of an artistic God, who utilised His voice to bring creation into existence, then maybe our words possess more power than we think. It is certainly true that, as our words are absorbed by others, they can generate feelings of encouragement and strength, or of dismay and fear. A casual negative comment can ruin a perfectly good day, and vice versa. It is a well-accepted theory that words spoken into the life of a child can influence and mould their character, and ultimately their success, in many areas beyond childhood.

As precious children of almighty God, our simple vocabulary is more important and holds more influence than we realise. As we proclaim statements of truth, we appear to have the capacity to help ourselves and others to nurture faith, build belief and foster conviction, drawing us constantly towards a greater understanding of God's endless love for us. So, as a community of women, with God's help, we try to shy away from flippant, negative black humour that is so prevalent in our culture. We call each other to account should we overhear a fellow believer scold and chastise themselves with a title less than that which God would afford them, and we take every opportunity to speak truth and encouragement to each other and ourselves. In this way, we are bringing God's goodness and reflecting God's nature with our voices, audible demonstrations of the glory of God, all the time exercising attributes we were destined to display.

The seductive voice of the devil stripped Eve of trust and belief in her heavenly Father, but God has always fostered a great desire towards His precious creation. No matter the harm rendered by the devil, God is able and willing to reverse this destructive power. He longs for us to develop the important skill of rejecting lies which lead to a diminished existence; to courageously proclaim the truths of God which guide us towards faith, an enlarged understanding of His love for us and the fulfilment of our eternal destiny. This powerful, effectual act leads the speaker along stepping stones to God-given freedom.

WHAT DOES GOD SAY ABOUT YOU?

Take some time to reflect on the following biblical truths:

You are a saint.	Ephesians 1: 1
You are someone in whom I now dwell.	1 Corinthians 3: 16
You are my friend.	John 15: 15
You are at peace with me.	Romans 5: 1
You are my child.	John 1: 12
You are a member of my Holy Nation.	1 Peter 2: 9
I tenderly love you.	Jeremiah 31: 3
You are now blameless in my presence.	Colossians 1: 22
You are able to approach my throne and ask for my help.	Hebrews 4: 16
You will never be condemned again.	Romans 8: 1
You are an heiress of the inheritance of Christ.	Romans 8: 17
You are united with my Son.	1 Corinthians 6: 17

You are royalty.	1 Peter 2: 9
You are my sweet aroma.	2 Corinthians 2: 15
You are now complete in my Son.	Colossians 2: 10
You belong to my Kingdom Of Light.	Colossians 1: 13
You are one of my chosen ones.	1 Peter 2: 9
You are a child of the Light.	1 Thessalonians 5: 5
You are salt and light.	Matthew 5: 13-14
You are justified.	Romans 5: 1
You are my ambassador.	2 Corinthians 5: 20
You are totally forgiven.	Colossians 1: 14
You are new, your old self was crucified.	2 Corinthians 5: 17 Romans 6: 6
You are my beloved.	Song of Songs 7: 10
You are my adopted child.	Galatians 4: 4-6
You are someone I rejoice over.	Zephaniah 3: 17
I know you completely.	Psalm 139: 1

	I chose you before the foundation of the world.	Ephesians 1: 4
	You are unique.	2 Corinthians 10: 12
	You have the mind of Christ.	1 Corinthians 2: 16
	You are not timid; you are full of love, power and self-control.	2 Timothy 1: 7
	You are more valuable to me than sparrows.	Matthew 10: 31
	You were made in my beautiful image.	Genesis 1: 27
	You are wonderfully and fearfully made.	Psalm 139: 14
	You are crowned with glory and honour.	Psalm 8: 5
	Sin no longer dominates your life.	Romans 6: 11
	By my grace you are now saved.	Ephesians 2: 8
	No-one or nothing will ever stop me loving you.	Romans 8: 38-39
	You are totally secure.	John 10: 29

SIGNPOSTS AND STEPPING STONES

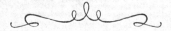

But you are a chosen people,
a royal priesthood, a holy
nation, God's special possession,
that you may declare
the praises of Him who called
you out of darkness and into
His wonderful light.

1 Peter 2: 9 (NIV)

ADAM'S AGONY

Adam reached out his hand as Eve passed him the newly broken piece of fruit. From its single bite mark, he could already smell its sweetness, begin to almost taste its flesh. Even as it touched his lips, Adam felt a shift, a dimension change; something in the foundations of the world had altered. With each increased pressure of his bite, the change in atmosphere became more intense, more powerful. Slowly, it began to build, to the point when it became unbearable and, almost impulsively, Adam released his prize and let it fall, hitting the floor with the mass of a giant stone. At that point, Adam became aware that the air around the Garden had become deathly still, as if all creation had paused and held its breath.

Then it overwhelmed him like a tidal wave. A crashing sensation of confusion, desolation, anguish and barrenness, an agonising medley of wretched emotions he never even comprehended before. Looking into Eve's eyes, he knew she was experiencing the same. There was no space to think or reason, he had no framework on which to build these new experiences and emotions. All he knew was that he felt exposed, humiliated and naked. He wanted to run away and hide, to cover up his body, which suddenly seemed so vulnerable and disgraceful.

As quickly as he could, he gathered together armfuls of fig leaves from nearby trees and, with fumbling fingers and shaking hands, he sewed them together to form a garment. Glancing across to Eve, he realised she had impulsively done the same. The outer covering strangely gave some relief to his sense of shame but inside, his heart was reeling. How could Eve have *been so foolish as to eat from the forbidden tree? Why had he followed her? What had they done? What had they done?*

(Paraphrased from Genesis 3: 6-7)

BECKY'S STORY

For many years, I believed that I wasn't made beautiful in the same way that my friends were. This lie had taken a grip on my life and controlled my everyday thinking and actions far more than I ever realised. From the moment I woke up, I would look in the mirror and analyse my body from head to toe. My mood was then the result of how many spots I could count on my face, how comfortable or tight my jeans fit, usually in a negative and pessimistic way.

Subconsciously, I think I was angry at God for allowing me to suffer from acne, as all my friends seemed to have moved on from this following their teenage years. Sometimes I would want to avoid social situations altogether and hide, unless I had enough time to cover up my acne with layers of makeup to try and mask what I knew was still there.

Other than God, my husband was the only one who saw the real impact that this had upon my life. I wouldn't dare tell others how I truly felt about myself, as that would just attract more attention to the parts of my body which I hated in so many ways. Then one evening as a team of women, we gathered together and, before God and each other, made ourselves vulnerable. We started being honest about the lies we knew had a hold on us and sought God to reveal to us areas in our lives that didn't reflect His glory. This was the first time I had spoken out loud to anyone other than my husband about the lie I had kept hold of for so many years.

I was then challenged by these women to make myself vulnerable before a large group of ladies at a church event and be honest about my struggles, in the hope that it would challenge others struggling with similar thought patterns. This seemed like the scariest thing in the world to do, but somehow I did it and the response was so accepting, loving and encouraging.

The truth is, I can still have negative thoughts about myself from time to time, but the difference is that I now recognise these are just lies and I find I have the strength to give these thoughts over to God; they are not mine to carry around with me. I can be honest with others if I am struggling, and allow them to pray for me. Also, I can now pop to the shops without having to apply a face full of makeup and I don't feel the need to hide away!

I am who I am; I am God's beautiful, chosen one.

Chapter 16

THE METAMORPHOSIS OF EVE

If lies had been the seeds planted in the soil of Eve's mind, then the fruit of those seeds was a change to her emotions and behaviour. Deceived by the devil and convinced that God was no longer trustworthy, Eve took fruit from the forbidden tree and a breathtaking metamorphosis took place.

Now, standing in the Garden, she was faced with the consequences of her actions and was overwhelmed by a sense of unexplained emotion. She became aware that she was naked. She had always been naked and she had never sensed the need to conceal her own perfectly created body before, but suddenly it had become so glaringly obvious. Even with her novice concept of sin, Eve instinctively understood that she was now flawed and could not remain exposed. Innocence was gone and was replaced by a self-consciousness that had previously been absent. Where once she was nude and felt no disgrace, now she must conceal her true self and shroud her nakedness. Where once she knew complete freedom and liberty, suddenly she felt unnaturally drawn towards camouflage and disguise.

Awkward and agitated in her own skin she reached for the foliage of a nearby fig tree and created for herself an apron made from leaves. Not a bikini of three small pieces of greenery as is so often depicted by artists, but a substantial garment to cover, hide and protect. What could have possibly been Eve's motivation for such a drastic response? The Bible is clear and reveals to us that, where once Adam and Eve were not ashamed, now the sensation was overpowering. Where once there was no shame, now this new emotion was present, and where shame dwells, other horrors lurk.

When the devil lied to Eve and drew her away from the voice of her heavenly Father, he knew there would be eternal consequences. He also knew that those consequences would carry a profound personal impact on every human who ever walked the face of the Earth. Listening to lies from the outside changes us on the inside. And so, when Eve believed the lies of the devil, it altered and distorted her forever. The perfect reflection of the almighty God she once carried was marred and, instead of internal peace and serenity, there was a raging conflict. These were emotions that she had never suffered before, strange and unpleasant sensations forcing her to act in a way which was totally alien to the woman she used to be. It was as if a giant door had opened wide, giving rite of passage to harrowing and distressful thoughts and feelings, emotions that made her feel vulnerable and unsafe, the distance she had chosen to place between herself and her God plunging her into an ocean of turmoil and confusion.

And so, sadly, along with the lies of the devil, shame entered the world, this rancid and destructive emotion wedging an unnatural distance between Eve and almighty God and reducing His treasured creation to so much less than she was intended to be. Yet even at that moment, the eternal love of her heavenly Father was already compelling Him to put into place the plan that would restore His beautiful creation to Himself. It could have been so different. If God had ever intended to abandon humanity to their newly acquired fate, He would have done so at the point of Eve's withdrawal of true self, at the second when she withered and shrunk behind a barrier of intertwined fig leaves.

But the nature of God is restoration, compassion and love and He is unable to act in any other way than to be true to Himself. God saw beyond the vision of the broken Eve that lay before His eyes, His omniscience tracing each perfectly placed flagstone along a pathway of redemption. His focus resting on the image of humanity returned to their true likeness; a people reclaimed. His precious creation once again abundantly reflecting His stunning purity and splendid glory.

Chapter 17

THE TRAMPOLINE

L ike many children born in the United Kingdom, I progressed from a small primary school to the 'big school' at the age of eleven and so commenced my secondary school education. It was an intimidating experience. Great Barr Comprehensive School was not only massive in size, but going there meant I had to learn to navigate different classrooms, follow a complex timetable and abide by a daunting number of new school rules. I was somewhat overwhelmed and just a little terrified! However, not everything about the secondary school was negative. They had an extensive number of extracurricular activities to explore, from learning a previously undiscovered talent such as netball or playing the violin, to improving an academic skill such as French or Mathematics; the choices appeared vast. The option that attracted my attention was trampolining. I had visions of being able to tumble and turn, tuck and straddle, with the grace and ease of elegance in motion.

However, there was a problem. In order to be considered for the trampolining club, you had to own a pair of regulation black school knickers. It's hard to comprehend now, but my childhood was so marked with extreme poverty that to request an additional item of school uniform was tantamount to requesting a piece of the moon. Either my mum genuinely could not afford them or the trampolining club was not high enough on her agenda; either way, the weeks went by and, despite my desperate pleas, the request remained denied. So, in the end, I decided to take matters into my own hands. Sneaking into my eighteen-year-old sister's bedroom one day, I rummaged through her drawers until I discovered what I believed to be a suitable piece of trampolining underwear.

How wrong I was.

That Thursday lunchtime, and with some apprehension, I took my place around the trampoline with all the other girls and waited for my name to be called, indicating it was my turn to mount the elevated mat. I climbed aboard and stood on the central cross where all trampolinists commence their routines. Slowly, keeping my head held high and my back straight, I began to bounce. As expected, my body, arms and gym skirt began to rise with each new spring. Suddenly I became aware of the titters of laughter that were circulating amongst my peers below. Desperately aware that my lacy knickers were less than acceptable to the group, I pressed on with gusto and tried to impress. With all the energy I could muster, I pulled my legs to forty-five degrees and attempted a seat drop, landing on my bottom and returning to an upright position. However, the lace of my sister's knickers had cruelly caught on the weave of the trampoline fabric, causing them to snag. Combine this detail with the fact that the knickers were several sizes too large for me and the inevitable happened. Cheeks revealed for all to see. My humiliation was complete.

I left the gym that day in floods of tears, any resemblance of pride in tatters, and thoroughly chastised myself for being so foolish. I could look back on that incident and smile at the foolish and naive ways of a rather desperate, soon-to-be teenage girl, if it wasn't for the fact that it was yet another episode in my life that added to all the years of pain, neglect and abuse, a history that resulted in me carrying a fundamental, internal and integral sense of shame.

Chapter 18

THE SPREAD
OF SHAME

In today's complex world, shame is a universally experienced emotion of epidemic proportions. It is encountered in all cultures, by all ages and by people from all walks of life. Shame is not gender-specific and occurs regardless of faith, sexuality or social status. Shame is understood to be a deeply unpleasant feeling which causes emotional distress. It is associated with equally untasteful emotions such as humiliation and disgrace.

Shame is not the same as guilt, although both occur when a person acts in a way that contradicts their own personal understanding of that which we know to be true and correct. When we proceed in a manner which opposes our own values and beliefs, we find ourselves feeling uncomfortable and embarrassed. Guilt says, 'I should not have done that; it was wrong.'. However, shame is something quite different. Shame is an emotion carried deep within the soul. It occurs when we look at our incorrect behaviour and attitude and come face to face with the fact that we are not who we thought we were; we are essentially flawed. Shame says, 'I should not have done that. It was a mistake but it doesn't surprise me that I acted that way. I always do. It's my nature, I am defective, I am wrong.'.

For some people, like Eve, shame occurs because of a single devastating incident which leaves a person feeling fundamentally filthy and unclean. It can be an act which they perpetrate or the vile behaviour of another acted upon them. However, shamefulness does not have to be attained instantly, it can occur over a period of time. Years of guilt, failure and disappointment begin to saturate a person's soul convincing them that there is something essentially wrong with them. Constant criticism and abuse, neglect and abandonment, can all lead to an identity dominated by the belief that a person is useless or insignificant. This toxic belief infiltrates a person's identity and they begin to consider themselves to be worthless and of no value to themselves or anyone else. Their self-worth essentially left in devastating tatters, shame inevitably moves in.

Society does nothing to help negate our pain. Unrealistic expectations of beauty, impractical goals of perfectly-presented children, immaculate homes and the constant drive for women to reach the top of the corporate ladder, leave us feeling inadequate and exhausted. Caught in the headlights of unattainable excellence, we look at our lives and shake our heads in disbelief. We are so much less than everybody requires us to be; we are simply not enough.

At its most superficial, shame can present with the softest touch, a gentle blush of a cheek or an uncomfortable shuffle in a chair. We smile to ourselves, move on as quickly as possible, urging the moment to pass. But at its pinnacle, shame leaves you feeling as if you inhabit a cage. The anguish can be so great that it compels you to throw yourself against the bars over and over again until you fall back, broken and wounded from your self-inflicted injuries. The despair of shame can leave you feeling so vulnerable that you strike out in anger against those you love the most. It leaves you with a sense of inferiority around peers and a constant disappointment with achievements. There is an underlying feeling of disapproval of even your most virtuous actions and an overwhelming sense of weakness every time you have to ask others for help. Mostly, there is an inability to consider yourself worthy of anything, from the mildest compliment to the deepest love, as shame notifies you, mind body and soul, that you are simply insufficient, as you are, to receive it.

This devastating state of heart and mind is a world away from the person God created us to be, but it is the destination of anyone who is constantly exposed to the lies of the devil. Shame is one of the devil's 'end games'. In a state of shamefulness, we fail to dazzle and shine as God created us to. And God, whose love for us is eternal and unchanging, formulates a plan for our deliverance; a plan devised in His brilliant mind before the world began.

"

The biggest disease today is not leprosy or tuberculosis, but rather the feeling of being unwanted."

Mother Teresa

Chapter 19

THE SEPARATING
POWER OF SHAME

Some years ago, during our annual Ladies Day Away, I invited the delegates to turn to the person next to them and say one positive thing about the person sitting on the adjacent seat. If they were already friends, then it could be a personal compliment, but if the person was a stranger, I invited them to make a pleasant comment about an item of clothing or a particular part of the stranger's appearance that they liked. The suggestion caused quite a stir. The room became full of awkward glances and nervous giggles. At the end of the exercise, I asked how many women had found it difficult to hear the positive compliment they had been paid. Most of the women in the room raised their hands. This activity revealed a startling truth. Most of the people attending that day felt they were not worthy of the compliment paid to them; many women in the room carried shame.

They were not alone. At the heart of the lie that I once believed, the lie that informed me that I was unlovable, lay an overwhelming blanket of shame. It was born out of so many of the lies I had been told as a child. Words were spoken over me that convinced my soul that I was useless, vile and pathetic. It was all part of the devil's cunning scheme. He knew that those lies would mercilessly ruin any wholesome view I held of myself, and any perception of God's goodness. He also fully expected me to respond in exactly the same pitiful manner as Eve. Like many before me, I turned my face from my loving God, cast my eyes down and cowered behind a well-constructed camouflage of charade and pretence. In this way, the devil hoped that my connection with God would be lost forever.

This is because shame delivers a devastating blow to relationships. It convinces us that in our current state, we are undesirable and undeserving of another's warmth, approval and affection. As such we find ourselves suspicious, believing that those who offer kindness towards us do so with ulterior motives. We secretly fear that any attempt to connect with us is made out of pity, duty or simply because they require something in return. It is a desolate and lonely place to exist. Without realising it, we become convinced that we are too damaged to ever be accepted by our peers and too repulsive to ever truly be loved by them. Should they catch sight of our flaws, we respond with anger, often blowing the whole comment out of proportion. In our hearts, we are quite certain that, if those around us were ever to be truly exposed to our authentic nature, they would firmly reject us and we would be alone forever.

And so, like many others before and after us, we learn to 'play the game'. We train ourselves to speak, dress and act in a manner that will be tolerable to those we long to be accepted by. Slowly, as the years go by, we become less and less the person we truly are and more and more the person we believe everybody wants us to be. Frankly, this masquerade is exhausting.

Like Eve, we work hard at creating an elaborate and complex barrier to conceal and hide our true selves. But this coping mechanism carries unforeseen consequences. Without even realising it we become confined, sacrificing our God-given freedom and liberty for the safety of our own prison. There, we can be tormented by a sense of loneliness and isolation, a deep soul-wrenching pain of disconnection and abandonment that we cannot explain. Equally, we live in constant terror that a flippant word or a negative attitude will bring the whole complicated barricade crashing down, leaving us exposed and defenceless.

However, the real act of tragedy comes as shame strips us of our ability to truly commune with God Himself. It is the most violent consequence of both the lies we believe and the shame that we unwittingly embrace. This situation is one which the jealous and passionate love of God is simply unwilling to tolerate. Drawing on all His creative power, He constructs a route, a pathway back into the loving arms of Himself, even though He is fully aware it will cost Him dearly.

Chapter 20

THE APEX OF EXISTENCE

When the devil lied to Eve, his motivations were unquestionably despicable. His desire was to reduce God's precious creation to a mere spectre of God's design and to fracture the glorious image we were created to reflect. In this way, he intended to rob us of our ability to relate to others, stealing from us the very thing he knew would afford us the most joy and satisfaction in life. However, the greatest act of thievery comes when shame assaults our ability to relate to God Himself.

Without remorse, shame screams the vile and dreadful lie that we are not good enough to receive the love and mercy of our devoted heavenly Father. After all, of all the beings in the universe, we are acutely aware that God above sees and comprehends all things. He is unrivalled in His ability to understand us and with Him there are no secrets, no misunderstandings and no redacted lines from our life's biography. That being the case, if we believe we are less than we should be, if our soul is impregnated and saturated with the rancid and poisonous presence of shame, then we will struggle to receive His forgiveness and we will wrestle to receive His love. We believe ourselves unable to embrace it; we consider ourselves unworthy to receive it.

As we grapple with our flawed selves, we are vulnerable to the devil's lies. We hear the gentle whisper, 'How could God possibly ever forgive you, you haven't changed. You can fool other people on the outside but on the inside, you're still your unreliable, unfaithful self', and, 'Who were you to approach God in worship this morning? You wish you could be one of those amazing Christians who has it all together, but you know you are not.' So quickly, almost subconsciously, we assemble our barrier of religiosity in the hope that our more presentable self will be allowed into the presence of our holy God and our Christian community, while all the time despising its presence, knowing it only achieves the very opposite to our intentions, desperate to see it crumble and powerless to know how.

In this state, shame robs us of a God-given gift which is essential to our God-reflecting nature; the profound and beautiful connection between ourselves and almighty God, between ourselves and other human beings. These relationships bring a level of satisfaction unparalleled by anything else we will ever experience. They are the apex of our existence; the sole reason God created us.

We were created to commune with the God who simply adores us and to connect with the family of humanity, to love without hesitation and to be loved without defence. And in doing so, we fully reflect the glory of the triune God, who exists in perfect harmony and connection with Himself.

God, in His infinite love for us, is fully aware of the plight of His beloved creation. He is not a passive God, neither indifferent to our situation nor unsympathetic to our emotional poverty. He beckons us again to be the women He created us to be. With each beat of His enormous heart, God is longing for us to recognise His desire to connect fully with us again. Walking closely by our side, He invites us to take the steps which release us from our captivity and bring us freedom to reflect His most foundational essence - His love. Written within the pages of His Holy Scriptures lies the antidote to the venomous lies of the devil which lead to shame; the gentle remedy to the broken hearts of humanity.

Chapter 21

THE HUMILIATION
OF CHRIST

When I was around thirty years old, I attended a 'Toronto Blessing' revival meeting in Sunderland. I remember at the end of the meeting we were asked by the leaders to stand in rows so we could receive prayer, but I didn't want to stand. I was sat on the floor so overawed with a sense of God's presence that I didn't want to move. I was caught up in His beauty and overwhelmed by His boundless love for me. Suddenly, I became aware of a voice deep within my soul. It was as if I could hear the audible voice of God and this is what He said to me. 'Shirley, I know what it feels like to be humiliated.' I was totally broken. It was as if someone had turned the key in an ancient lock and flung open a solid oak door. It was the first time anyone had ever articulated an emotion I knew lay at the core of my being. What's more, God could fully identify with me because

He had experienced abounding and unprecedented humiliation too during His years walking among His beloved creation.

When the precious son of God came to Earth, He was conceived out of wedlock, birthed in a filthy stable and cradled in a cattle's feeding trough. During His years He knew exile, hunger and anguish. He lived His life under constant threat of death by the religious leaders of His day, many of whom loathed and despised Him. He was constantly rejected, frequently disdained and brutally betrayed by people with whom He had meticulously invested years of His life.

When Jesus walked His final days here on the Earth, they were marked by humiliation, dishonour and contempt. He was escorted before a jeering crowd, who had once laid palm leaves at His feet, only to be greeted by obscenities as they called for His unrighteous execution. He was stripped naked and His body exposed and laid bare while a boned cat o' nine tails ripped the flesh from His back. As they tortured Him, His body became disfigured and mutilated. They taunted Him to 'save Himself' as He had once saved others, laughing at His messianic claims as He grew weaker and weaker with each passing hour. They placed a crown of thorns upon His head as if to reinforce that His self-declared Kingdom was as fickle as tinder and as fleeting as chaff. Finally, they nailed Him to a wooden post, outside the city walls surrounded by thieves and fools. There they placed a mocking plaque above His breaking body, identifying Him as the soon-to-be demised King of the Jews.

The plan of God was always going to be deeply personal. It was never going to be a series of orders issued in isolation from a distant, dusty ministerial office.   God's plan was always going to involve Him standing on the front line with His people, giving something substantial of Himself to the cause, being willing to bear the same burden, even unto death.

The humiliation that Jesus experienced immersed Him in so many of the occurrences which have perpetuated our own shame.   He was frequently exposed to many of the heartbreaking experiences and practices which propagate a sense of worthlessness and leave us feeling unloved and unlovable.   He fully identified with our pain. And yet during His years on Earth, He never once displayed the behaviour of someone whose life was saturated with shame.   He never once displayed any signs of being hidden or separated from His Father God ... that is, right up until the moment that He hung on the cross.   There Jesus demonstrated the fullness of the consequences of shame in their entirety.   That single moment echoing another momentous second in the history of the world, as a singular pinnacle when everything changes.   Shame may have entered the world in the shape of a piece of forbidden fruit, growing on a prohibited tree in the Garden of Eden but the doorway for its departure came in the shape of a wooden cross, standing outside a city wall, in a place called Calvary.

"

There is a beautiful transparency
to honest disciples who never wear
a face and do not pretend to be
anything but who they are.'

Brennen Manning

Chapter 22

THE STEP OF
AUTHENTICITY

As a group of women, we have been so humbled by God's incredible commitment to us as we walk this life-changing journey. God has taken our hands and guided us down unfamiliar pathways, exposing how we were caught in the headlights of destructive lies and shame that have their roots in humanity's first lady. None of us would say we have 'arrived' at the final destination, but we have taken careful steps, in line with the Bible's directives.

One of these directives has impacted us all; its name is authenticity.

Authenticity is the art of being genuine, vulnerable and transparent. It's the decision to step away from the historic apron of protection we have erected around ourselves and reveal our true being; the dynamic act of choosing to remove the barriers we have consciously or subconsciously created and instead exhibit our true inner self for others to see. Authenticity is the art of being sincere and candid about who we really are and then allowing others contact with our genuine heartfelt thoughts and responses. It's the act of being honest about the way we really perceive things, rather than simply saying what we believe others expect us to say. It's the ability to act out of our deepest convictions irrespective of the possible consequences.

It's a daring approach. It requires a mindful decision to expose ourselves; a decisive deliberate choice. But most of all, it requires an enormous, unprecedented level of courage.

Authenticity is a critical step in the demolishing of the stronghold of shame. It shatters the doors of our concealment, demolishing their solidity and tearing from the walls the hinges of lies that hold them in place. All the years of confinement, all the weight of secrets and heaviness, of pretence, is suddenly released and we are liberated. Like lancing an enormous abscess, the relief is painful, overwhelming and yet strangely welcome.

Then with burning intensity, authenticity allows the light to burst into the cold greyness of our cell, permeating every corner. For it is at that moment that we discover an astonishing truth; God's unstoppable, unchangeable and immeasurable love and acceptance of us is available to us, even in the light of our imperfections. The love and desire for communion with humanity never left God when Eve ate the forbidden fruit and it doesn't leave Him when we fail and disobey Him now. We are eternally surrounded and saturated by the love of God ... if we would only allow ourselves to receive it. It is a certainty we will never be able to test and discover unless we are brave enough to expose our true selves and wait for God's response. The Bible tells us that it was while we were in our sinful state that the love of God compelled Him to die for us.

It's hardly surprising that this courageous act holds such power because authenticity is a modern, western word which is strikingly similar to an ancient biblical term, 'confession'. Confession does not exist for God's benefit. He does not need to hear us tell Him of our weaknesses and failures - He is already aware of them. In the same way, as God knew where Adam and Eve were in the Garden and the reason for their act of betrayal, God knows all things. Confession forces us to be authentic with ourselves and to admit the truth of our own heart, mind and actions.

Stopping us in our tracks, confession reveals an inner acknowledgement of weakness and inadequacy, a vulnerability that exposes us. But its power does not simply lie there. Being authentic with another allows our true inner self, the one we so struggle to love and accept, to be loved and accepted by others. It exposes our inner soul and opens the way for warmth and compassion to be poured into the darkest recesses of our being. It creates a space where we can receive nourishing, wholesome validation and approval and it constructs a platform where we can hear words we so long to hear. 'You are OK, you are enough'. In short, authenticity and confession destroy the premise for shame.

This important step of confession was never a means of God to expose us and humiliate us, rather it is His gift to us. For it is when we confess our sinful state to God that we are flooded with His gracious response of mercy, forgiveness, love and acceptance.

This generous invitation comes to us from the passionate heart of a God who loves us and desires that we are fully restored. He longs for us to be authentic with ourselves, each other and our God, fracturing the apron we hide behind and destroying its concealing power. Exposed and vulnerable, our truthful self is laid bare, opening the way for us to experience His immense love for us and returning us to the intimacy we were destined to know. These inaugural steps along the path of freedom were designated for us before the world began.

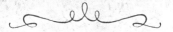

Surely He took up our pain and bore
our suffering, yet we considered Him punished
by God, stricken by Him, and afflicted.
But He was pierced for our transgressions,
He was crushed for our iniquities;
the punishment that brought us peace was on
Him, and by His wounds we are healed.
We all, like sheep, have gone astray, each
of us has turned to our own way; and the
Lord has laid on Him the iniquity of us all.

Isaiah 53: 4-6 (NIV)

RACHEL'S STORY

I have known God for many years, but despite 'knowing' lots of things about being a Christian, I thoroughly believed the lie that I needed to work hard in order to be a good Christian, and it permeated all of my life. I don't think I would have said at the time that I felt God was displeased with me when I got things wrong, because I knew that this was not biblical, but actually, looking back, I certainly did believe it and lived it. As a result, I did an awful lot of intense striving and had really lost the joy of what it is to know God. I was actually bored with being a Christian because there was little excitement about knowing God. This lie also led me to want to be perfect at whatever I did and, as a result, I was desperate for people to compliment me when I got something right, and devastated if I received any kind of criticism.

A few years ago, I was in an environment where I learnt what it was to bask in God's love. It sounds awfully simple and there is nothing new in what I am about to say but, bit by bit, I asked God to show me more of His love for me. I thought I already knew what it was to be loved by God, that I had always known God as my Father but, all of a sudden, I was beginning to know that not only was God my Father, but I was also, therefore, His beloved child, His precious daughter. I began to newly experience the pleasure of God, and it was good and light and fun, and totally not dependent on me! God loves me. Simple really. He adores me, thinks I am amazing, dances and spins with delight over me with outrageous and very loud singing. It didn't happen overnight but over a period of about a year, spending time loving God and feeling His love in a fresh and new way was like experiencing a revolution in my life. I now know a new lightness, and I experience heaps more joy. I laugh in His presence because I know that I haven't earned that love and nothing I do wrong will ever take that away. I can blow it, and frequently do, but God still loves me passionately and completely.

It is incredibly freeing to know that God loves me no matter what. I now know that whatever I do - whether it's about being a parent to my kids or serving at church - I just have to open my ears to hear the applause of Heaven. For some things I do, I don't even look to see what others think of how I am doing - if I get a compliment from someone, it's a bonus and not a necessity, because I know God's pleasure. For other things I do, especially personal things like being a mum and a wife, I have to really remind myself of this truth and to battle the old lie. But it doesn't change the truth that God loves me no matter what.

The truth is that being a Christian is not meant to be a drudge, it is meant to be full of joy. I have more courage to try new things and to step out of my comfort zone now, and I am loving the adventure of that because I can remind myself that God loves me before I even attempt anything for Him. I am seeing this truth slowly permeate every area of my life and it is erasing the effects of that lie that I once believed. Knowing God is meant to give me a life that is abundant because God loves me. So simple, so deeply profound and so easy to miss!

Chapter 23

THE INNATE
KNOWLEDGE OF EVE

When Eve listened to the lies of the devil and ate the forbidden fruit, shame caused her to hide her distorted and sinful self from her loving God. This is a pattern that has been present in so many of our lives ever since. However, in the sending of His son, Jesus, to dwell among us on Earth, God fully identified with us, exposing Himself to the very experiences which perpetuate shame and carrying them with Him to be nailed to the cross in an act of absolute commitment and complete sacrifice. Shame has no place in the life of a believer. Jesus took it all. However, there was another dimension at play in this earth-shattering scenario.

I once heard someone call 'pain' one of life's 'little, unpleasant experiences'. Clearly, they had never been through childbirth! An encounter with pain can range from a mildly insignificant headache to the rages of anguish and agony; all thoroughly disagreeable. And yet without this strange, nerve-driven sensation, we would be in mortal peril because, for all its discomfort, pain protects us. It reminds us that our bodies are fragile and easily damaged. It also informs us, in no uncertain terms, that something is physically wrong with us, drawing our attention to the part of our anatomy which is struggling to function as it should.

In the same way, God created humanity with a sensation which points to injury and dysfunction deep within our souls. It is a powerful, innate response that informs us we have acted in a manner which is alien to the person God created us to be. When our thoughts, words and deeds fail to reflect the heart of our gracious and loving heavenly Father, in whose perfect image we were created, a cautionary emotion is experienced deep within our being. This awareness is known as guilt and it occurs as a result of our God-given sense of justice.

When God created Eve, He fashioned her in the image of His magnificent self. She was formed to reflect every aspect of His chaste nature and that included His untainted virtue and perfect sense of justice. Sewn within the fabric of her very being lay an impression of God's own character; enveloped in her very essence existed the imprints of a righteous creator. Now in the Garden of Eden, Eve was faced with her unrighteous act; she had eaten of the forbidden fruit and she intuitively recognised that she had done wrong. Time did not pass as the reality began to sink in, nor did she require someone to explain to her that she had committed an act of infidelity. Eve simply knew.

Guilt is not like shame; it is more rational and objective. Whilst the sensation of shame informs that we are less than we should be, guilt informs us that we have responded with unrighteousness. We find ourselves suddenly conscious that our attitude or behaviour does not reflect our moral code. We have acted unjustly. We have not acted in a fashion in line with the person we are meant to be. We have done something wrong. It may be that we have lied or been unreasonably angry over a minor incident, but most likely we have encroached upon our most sacred connection and our actions have harmed or offended someone else.

Though guilt may leave us feeling distressed and disappointed with ourselves, it exists to draw attention to the desecration of our internal boundaries and our God-given sense of righteousness. Just as pain is meant to cause us to withdraw our hand from a harmful flickering flame, so guilt always existed to lead us away from an immoral path and into purity.

66

'My deepest awareness of myself
is that I am deeply loved by
Jesus Christ and I have done
nothing to earn or deserve it.'

Brennan Manning

Chapter 24

THE JUSTICE OF GOD

aught off guard by a rising tide of distasteful emotion, saturated by a sense of shame and conscious of her guilt, Eve suddenly became aware of aspects of the nature of God which she had never particularly noticed before. It's not that God had changed, after all Eve recognised perfectly well that God was the most constant of all the beings in the Universe. His love, tenderness and goodness were still glaringly obvious. But now His holiness seemed to shine more radiantly than she had ever realised in the past. So much so that it almost wounded her. It was if she now existed in the shadows, looking into a place of brilliant, searing light, a perspective entirely altered from the one she had when she dwelled in the light with Him; her own now unclean and polluted self so devastatingly obvious in contrast.

What's more, Eve felt subject to a facet of the temperament of God she had never experienced before. She alarmingly encountered the wrath of God, His unequivocal righteous anger at her decision to disobey Him and her choice to violate their most sacred agreement. Just like all the other attributes, almighty God's wrath had always been part of His complex and beautiful character. After all, God is a holy and just being. To love without ferocity would make His love weak and soppy and to judge without passion and wrath would make His holiness shallow and insipid. Eve's actions had provoked the disapproving yet virtuous judgement of her Father God. He still adored her, still longed for her to be all that He had created her to be. But now something had shifted in the closeness of their relationship. Eve was exposed like never before to His righteous anger, the natural consequence of God's perfect morality; a code she had recklessly broken.

The justice of God carried in the heart of Eve now highlighted an inconsistency between them. Where once there was a unity of holiness and purity, now there was division. Where once there existed intimate connection, a shared form of light and righteousness, now all evidence of harmony and uniformity was shattered. Like tar and water, it was no longer possible for sacred coherence to exist between them.

It must have appeared to Eve that, on the surface, the separation of God and humanity had reached an impasse, a point of no return. Where once there was utter trust and connection between them, now there lay an ocean of distance, encompassing shifting waves of filth and guilt and an ebbing tide of shame. If only she stopped to remember that God never changes, that

His splendid nature is one of love and restoration; that His commitment to His creation is unfailing, unswerving and entirely dependable.

Humble yourselves, therefore,
under God's mighty hand, that
He may lift you up in due time.
Cast all your anxiety on Him
because He cares for you.

1 Peter 5: 6-7 (NIV)

Chapter 25

THE STEP OF HUMILITY

When I was a child, I was quite a tomboy. I spent many a happy hour climbing trees and swinging high on homemade ropes hung over tall branches. One fateful evening, I decided to do something that could have possibly killed me. I leaned across a waist-high metal rail with the intention of allowing my entire body to swing underneath it. The plan was that, after the end of the exploit, I would have landed in an upright position. It was a manoeuvre I had done a thousand times. What I failed to take into account, however, was that I had grown and therefore the distance between my waist and my head had become longer. With all the force I could muster I hurled myself around the bar in a forward movement and as gravity took hold my head swiftly hurled itself towards the ground, eventually hitting it with colossal force. The result was an enormous bruise, temporary memory loss and a severe concussion that left me bed bound for days. I learned an important lesson that day - our actions carry consequences!

For every choice and decision we make, there will always be an outcome. Eat too much chocolate and I'll never get into my size fourteen shorts this summer, drive too fast past a policeman with a speed camera and I'm certain to get a fine. Agree to take on too many tasks and I'm sure to do none of them well! It's as if God has written a law into the fabric of nature itself saying 'you reap what you sow'.

After Eve chose to disobey the command of God and eat from the tree of the knowledge of good and evil, she instinctively knew there would be consequences to her actions. The narrative informs us that she was afraid and fear, according to the Gospel of John, has its root in the anticipation of punishment. Eve knew that someone had to be held responsible for the act of unrighteousness that had taken place. There would be a punishment, a consequence of acting in a manner which violated her mandate to reflect the perfect glory of a holy God. That penalty would be death.

Death occurred in Eden in so many ways; the death of the beautiful, pure nature of Eve; the initiation of physical decline which impacted every living thing in existence; the separation of the bond between created being and Creator which had endured since her conception; the death of our precious God-ordained freedom.

The Book of Genesis tells us that, rather than taking responsibility for her own actions, Eve pitilessly projected the blame onto someone else. She charges the serpent with the crime, shifting the fault away from herself and complaining that he had deceived her. It must have been to her horror that Adam dealt with his guilt in the same foolish manner and Eve found herself on the receiving end of his accusations, condemned by the voice of the man who had once stood completely united with her.

This is a persuasive ploy that the devil has used on an unexpecting humanity ever since. He works tirelessly to try to convince us that we are not responsible for our own thoughts and actions. He persuades us that our poor choices and warped beliefs about ourselves, our God and our world, are the consequences of our deprived upbringing, our limited education and our influential friends. While these reasons may explain why we have listened to the devil's voice, believed his lies and lived our life in a manner that reflected them, they should never be used to excuse them.

In the heart of our loving heavenly Father, there is a burning passionate desire that we come to Him with honesty and humility. Acknowledging our failures and our flaws, admitting that we have been wrong to believe and act in a manner we were never created to do. This act of repentance both infuriates and terrifies the devil because he knows that it is another important step which is instrumental to regaining our freedom, a stepping stone along the pathway to our God-appointed destiny.

Chapter 26

THE REDEMPTION
OF EVE

Before I was a Christian believer, I was as guilty of betrayal as Eve. Not only had I treacherously listened to the voice of the devil and rejected the thoughts of God, I had lived a life totally incongruent to the one God created me to live. Hiding beneath my self-made canopy of shame, I had inadvertently disconnected myself from my heavenly Father and often, without even realising it, had rejected His purposes and designs for my life. Like Eve, I had become subject to the just and virtuous wrath of God; my unrighteous thoughts and deeds blatantly defiled in the light of His stunning holiness. In that fallen state, I was incapable of helping or redeeming myself and I was certainly in no condition to offer an adequate or plausible penance for my disgraceful transgressions. This is because the Bible is clear that all who have acted in a way contrary to the holiness of God are imperfect and subject to death. This imperfection made me unsuitable and woefully inadequate to release myself from the conviction of my own failings. I could not redeem myself; my defectiveness made me an unfit candidate. Only a being that is not subject to the conviction of sin could pay the penalty for it.

And so our precious heavenly Father, whose heart towards us has never changed, reveals His immense longing and passion for reconnection with His beloved creation. Saturated in mercy and tenderness, God delivers humanity by paying the penalty for our sinfulness Himself. He sends Jesus, His only Son, the perfect representation of the Godhead, and allows Him to carry the weight of our verdict. Our guilt became His guilt; our sinfulness became His sinfulness; our punishment became His punishment. Then, after completing the sentence of our conviction through His death on the cross, Jesus returns to His Father in Heaven, marked by the cost of His sacrifice for eternity.

Of all the lies that we could surrender to, the falsehood that the death of Jesus is irrelevant to our lives and for our current situation is the most damning of all. The devil would dearly love to snatch from our hearts and minds the significance of this most beautiful and redeeming act; the act which reverses Eve's treachery in Eden; the act that God foresaw before the dawn of time; the act that would return God's treasured creation to Himself. The devil's desire is that we continuously dismiss God's most gracious deed because he knows that, through this, we are again made worthy to enter the presence of our loving heavenly Father without the barrier of shame. Because if we do not, we will be held captive to shame forever, believing that we are unworthy to know Him, since the price for our sins remains unpaid. It is because of Jesus' amazing undertaking that we are no longer condemned. We are worthy, not because of anything we have done, but because God has made us worthy. We are accepted, not because of our inadequate actions, but because God has made us acceptable. This is why we must turn our thoughts again and again to the cross because if we ever forget that the sacrifice of Jesus paid the price for our sinfulness, we will forever believe God is angry with us and that we remain objects of His wrath. This toxic image of God will rob us of ever believing that He is good and deprive us of ever receiving His unending love.

As a community of women, we are learning to allow ourselves to hold the same vision of ourselves as God has; redeemed, forgiven, accepted and desired by a God who simply adores us. For some, the leap has not been too far while for others it has felt like a thousand miles. Yet it simply changes everything once you have a hold of this truth. The way to God is wide open because God has made it so. Suddenly, the barriers we have erected to protect ourselves disintegrate like ice before the heat of the sun. That which has shrouded the doorway to an intimate relationship with God gently vanishes and we can walk through into the warmth and acceptance of His presence.

Chapter 27

THE STEP OF
FORGIVENESS

When Jesus Christ died at Calvary, He opened up a way for us to satisfy the cries of guilt that echo within our souls. He paid the price of our wrongdoing; thereby the justice of God is wholly satisfied. The deserving punishment that we were so rightly aware of is taken and executed on a Roman cross. But there is yet another consequence to this precious and powerful act of our loving God. It results in forgiveness.

When I was a young girl my stepfather's name for me was the 'Whore of Babylon'. It's a biblical term found in the last book of the Bible and, even in my fledgling years, I knew what the term implied. It was the personification of all that was repulsive and vile on the Earth, a blatant well-crafted image of all that was wicked and disgusting in the world. What is more, my stepfather had no hesitation in acting upon me some of the very behaviours that his chosen nickname suggested. Physical, emotional and sexual abuse, all performed with a careful, calculated measure of violence and resent-filled malice. By the time I reached my teenage years, I had come to believe so many untrue, damaging lies about myself. As such, I thought I was the 'scum of the earth', my heart and soul saturated in shame.

The bizarre thing is, when I became a Christian and finally realised that I needed to forgive my stepfather, it wasn't as difficult as you may expect. I don't for one second believe he was in any way justified in his action but, because he was my stepfather, I think that I felt he had no real responsibility to treat me well. There were no relational bonds or blood ties between us; he had no paternal vested interest in me. However, the same could not be said for my mother. I honestly believe that my mother endeavoured to love me with all her heart, but the death of my own father when I was just five years old had left her devastated. Depression and anxiety, coupled with her own burden of guilt and shame, meant she often felt overwhelmed. I have no memories of her ever perpetuating any of the abuse I experienced as a child, but she never stopped it either. She failed to adequately guard, defend and protect me and it was that failing that I found so intensely difficult to forgive.

Forgiveness is more that the act of letting go. It requires you to admit that a wrong has been committed and then to acknowledge that you will not condemn the person for it. When our righteous anger rises within us because a crime has been perpetuated, true forgiveness says, 'I will no longer punish you by withholding my love and favour'. I am not saying we should excuse the action. If my stepfather had still been alive today, it would have been right for him to be held accountable for the wrongdoing he committed and to be subject to the consequences of his depraved choices. However, I am saying we should choose to forgive the person.

When Jesus died on the cross, He paid the penalty for all the misdeeds we have ever committed in the past and will ever execute in the future. In this way, we are pardoned for our actions. The Bible tells us that, as a result, we are no longer under condemnation. However, the limitless mercy of God goes further. He entirely, completely and abundantly forgives us. This means that no matter what we have done or will do in the future, He never withholds His love and favour from us. His loving arms are always beckoning us, the pathway into the continuous warmth and presence is now wide open.

As children created in the image of a merciful God, He invites us to live a life which reflects His forgiving nature. To forgive those who have lied to us and placed us in situations which have perpetuated a sense of shame and worthlessness. This extensive company of people may include parents, teachers, colleagues, friends and family. And it may include you. Forgiving yourself of sins committed, for foolishly believing a lie and for wasting years of your life in condemnation and shame, is as important as forgiving anyone else. Releasing yourself from your own judgements of punishment and allowing yourself to love yourself and be kind to yourself again is essential if we are ever going to walk away from the pain of Eden, and if we are ever going to radiate God's glory and manifest His goodness.

As we allow ourselves to engage with the forgiveness of our tender loving God, recognising His mercy and accepting His redemptive kindness, so we are learning to release others; this important decision propels us beyond another precious milestone on the highway of freedom.

Praise the Lord, my soul,
and forget not all His benefits —
who forgives all your sins and heals
all your diseases, who redeems
your life from the pit and crowns
you with love and compassion,
who satisfies your desires with
good things so that your youth
is renewed like the eagle's.

Psalm 103: 2-4 (NIV)

THE BLAME GAME

Now, at last, the moment had arrived. Adam and Eve stood before almighty God, fearful and crestfallen, abysmal and dismayed. God longed for them to see in His eyes the tenderness and mercy that reflected His nature, but they could not even bring themselves to raise their heads and look at Him. He had called them out of hiding, wooing them softly and displaying all His affection in the tone and pitch of His profound voice, longing for them to return to Him willingly and humbly ... but it was too late.

Gently, God began to probe the circumstances around which the forbidden fruit was taken and trust between them broken. 'How had you found yourselves in this state?' 'Who had enticed you?' 'Where has the revelation of your nakedness come from?' Of course, God already knew all the answers; He was simply looking for a connection, giving them a pathway back to Himself.

As His once beautiful creation began to reply, the devastation of God's heart could not be measured. Instead of a soft response of sorrow, there was a brittle retort of defence. Instead of a display of longing to renew their bond of love and friendship, there was a selfish, self-serving display of reproach and blame. Without restraint, Adam and Eve hurled an array of accusations, each denouncing another and implicating the Creator and the created alike. There was no demonstration of repentance or remorse; no stolid acceptance of responsibility for the decisions taken or the implication that would ensue.

Slowly, God revealed the consequences of the day's events.

To the serpent, a change in physical form and a prediction of the devil's demise. To Eve, an increase in physical pain as she reproduces a humanity warped and marred by comparison to the one she was destined to birth. And to Adam, the revelation of the catastrophic consequences which will impact the Earth and all who dwell upon it.

(Paraphrased from Genesis 3: 8-19)

EMILY'S STORY

I used to believe that God would miss me out, that He had enough for others but never quite enough for me! I felt I was always at the bottom of His pile and that I saw others having amazing experiences of God, but that was never what happened for me. This made me feel like I was second-rate, but I would never have admitted that to anyone ... I hardly dared admit it to myself. I assumed that I had to accept that this was what it was always going to be like. I assumed I should just be happy with what God did for others and accept that that would not be my story.

This thought process made me withdraw. I tried to be happy when others had amazing experiences with God, but at the same time, I struggled inside myself to really be happy for them. Ultimately, this meant I limited what God wanted to do in my life and I had a barrier between myself and Him.

Then one day, I realised that I was basically living under a big lie and it occurred to me that it created a massive blockage between me and God! At a conference, God took me on an individual journey with Him - I didn't need to go forward for ministry and didn't need to have anyone pray with me. He showed me why I believed this lie that there was never enough for me ... all linked back to something that had happened in my life twenty-seven years previously! I had given this lie permission to affect how I saw things. I prayed through this whole situation, releasing forgiveness towards others and allowing God to show me how He 'always' had enough for me and that I was 'not' second rate!

I felt alive in a new way after this. I no longer compare what God is doing in others with what He is doing in me. My journey is individual with Him ... I am secure in that. I also know that there have been dramatic changes in the lives of the people I was able to forgive ... they know nothing about my journey, but there has been a change in them too!

I do sometimes still hear the old lie coming at me again, but I can throw that off now. This has also made me much more aware of what other lies I may be believing ... and as a result, I seek God as to what is the root of those lies when I am aware of them ... by dealing with the root, there is lasting change, rather than just squashing the lie down.

For I am the Lord your God
who takes hold of your right hand
and says to you,
Do not fear; I will help you.

Isaiah 41: 13 (NIV)

Chapter 28

IN THE SHADOW
OF FEAR

I am not afraid of many things. Large black hairy spiders, freezing cold water and that moment you touch down in an aeroplane ... scary stuff! Commonly, people's fears cover a multitude of things from fear of heights, fear of clowns, fear of flying, fear of dogs and, bizarrely in my opinion, fear of buttons! Some fear is instinctive, an innate inbuilt survival strategy. Other fears, however, come from past experiences and incidents. My fear of aeroplane touchdown, for example, was born after a particularly uncomfortable and disagreeable landing on a wet and windy runway in Belfast.

Some fears we encounter are almost universal. Fear of rejection by those around us, fear of failure and fear of spending our final years on Earth destitute of friendship and alone. It seems that, as we go about our everyday lives, fear is a constant shadow which follows us everywhere. This disagreeable, disdainful emotion is important because it can so often be the motivation for many of our actions. In fact, I have heard it said that as humans we only ever have two motivations for the decisions and exploits we take: love or fear. At the base of our options, it is these two powerful sentiments which inevitably inspire our choices. The difficulty is that no matter why we choose fear over love, the end result is always the same: disconnection.

Fear always results in, and emanates from, some level of disconnection. It disconnects us from our relationships and disconnects us from our destiny. In the case of Adam and Eve, it did both. In fear, their perfectly cohesive relationship became fractured as Adam criticised and lambasted Eve, refusing to take responsibility for his own actions. Friction now existed between them and their relationship became blemished and tainted. Now the perfect image of the harmony of the triune God that they had carried for so long was shattered. They were no longer able to fulfil their mandate to fill the Earth with those who perfectly reflected God's glory, their true destiny now impossible to achieve. Equally, their perfectly cohesive connection with their heavenly Father lay in tatters, as in fear they attempted to hide their brokenness before a holy and perfect God.

If we were to ask a psychologist the question, 'What is fear?', they would tell us that at its root, fear originates from one thing. Fear comes from a belief that we are being threatened; a sense of dread that we may be harmed. At its root, fear is the conviction that we are no longer safe. Before her unrighteous act, the experience of fear would have been absolutely alien to Eve. She would have lived her life in the Garden of Eden with no concept of danger or harm. There would never have been a moment when she felt in peril, vulnerable or threatened. Eve would have been completely secure in the knowledge that her heavenly Father was watching over her, providing for her, protecting her and sheltering her beneath the shadow of His presence ... right up until the moment she ate the fruit and everything changed. Suddenly, Eve became unsure of God's commitment to her; she sensed His anger at her disobedience and felt unworthy of His affection. Eve became afraid, and fear, according to the Gospel of John, had a source in the anticipation of punishment.

Feeling unsheltered for the first time in her existence Eve begins to act in a manner which reflects her lack of security. In her actions, we see a demonstration of an emotion now universal to us all.

Eve was insecure.

Chapter 29

THE VIA FERRATA

Some years ago, I went to France on holiday and whilst I was there I completed a 'Via Ferrata'. Let me explain. A Via Ferrata is basically a horizontal rock climb. You clamber down from the top of the cliff onto small metal rungs and you proceed to traverse the rock face suspended hundreds of feet above the ground. Now I have done some pretty crazy things in my life, but this one wins the gold star hands down. I have to say, my levels of anxiety went through the roof. It was unquestionably a 'TENA Lady moment'. The rungs were far too small; my feet were way too big. My little sweaty hands were gripping the rock so hard, I thought they would stay in that contorted shape forever. 'What were you thinking?', I kept chastising myself, 'Why do you get yourself in these situations, you crazy girl?'.

But the truth is I would do it all again in a heartbeat. Why? Because for as much as a fall would have caused me some serious cuts and grazes it would not have caused my death. You see, the term Via Ferrata means 'iron road' and it refers to the iron rail that runs the full length of the course to which you are firmly attached. I was nervous of falling, the pain of the injury and the humiliation were very real concerns, but I was able to continue my escapade because I had complete faith in the fixed iron cable and my harness which held me there.

When Eve disobeyed God, it was if she became disconnected from the invisible cord that had joined them together since the beginning of time. Suddenly, she felt exposed, vulnerable and adrift from the source of her strength and security.

It is no wonder that she felt compelled to hide, or that she felt afraid.

Since that day to this, every human child has been born with a prevailing sense of loss, a compelling deficiency of the soul which permeates everything. However, like someone born into a world of darkness, we do not necessarily recognise that we were created to exist in the light. All we know is that, deep down in our being, there is a voice calling out that there is more to this life than we are living. Great preachers have called it 'the God-shaped hole', the place of emptiness that can only be filled when we reconnect to God Himself.

Chapter 30

SILENCING THE FEAR

Throughout humanity, we have tried to silence our fears, create safety and satisfy our emptiness. For some people, this has become a catalyst for their reason for living, perpetuating their fear and detaching themselves from their true destiny. They tell themselves that as long as they have enough in their savings account and a pension to fall back on, they will be secure. As long as they present themselves with trendy clothes, an immaculate home and the latest bauble of success, they will be acceptable to those around them, thereby reducing the risk of rejection and conflict and remaining safe within the 'tribe'. They tell themselves that as long as they stay fit, eat the right food and exercise to the tenth degree they will avoid poor health and live forever.

Many people foolishly fill their world with noise and busyness, playing the radio in the car, wearing earphones on the street and keeping the TV on all day.

Actively running away from the void that exists within them and avoiding the absent presence they feel inside. Anything, in fact, to take their focus away from the fact that there is a painful hollowness deep within that has been there since as long as they can remember.

Eventually, many of us reach the conclusion that none of the above brings real security or lasting satisfaction. The only thing that brings some relief to the emptiness is relationships; warm, heartfelt friendships and deep, loving companionship. This is what most of us live for. To look into the eyes of another human being and experience a connection; to know them and be known by them brings a level of satisfaction beyond all material possessions. To have another by your side who believes in you, walks with you and defends you, brings a level of safety no well-filled bank account can provide. It's not surprising because as created beings, made in the image of one who relates, we were made to connect and relate to others with intimacy and tenderness.

However, there is a proverbial 'fly in the ointment'. The problem is that we are simply imperfect, as are those we come to love. As such, we fail each other. Helplessly we watch as our insecurities turn into quick, knee-jerk responses that bring pain and confusion to the ones we truly love. We take our own flawed, shame-filled selves and we try to love another with everything we have. In turn, those around us try to do the same, but conflict and mistrust have a habit of appearing in the most solid and loving of relationships. I am not saying it is not possible to love and receive love devoutly; I am saying it is impossible for us to love and receive love perfectly. Unrealistic expectations, unkind decisions brought about by life's pressures, lack of communication and an act which breaks trust, eventually wears away at the most sturdy friendship. The solid rock we thought we stood on suddenly shifts like sand beneath our feet. These sometimes daily, maybe rare, occurrences remind us that our security cannot be completely placed in any human, no matter how much we love them.

The Bible is clear that only perfect love casts out all fear.

Chapter 31

THE SOURCE OF PERFECT LOVE

When I walked the length of the cliff on my Via Ferrata, there would have been little point in my putting my faith in the cable which held me to the rock face if it contained fractures and frays. Only a strong, undamaged, complete cable would evoke my trust. And only perfect love can truly cast out our anxiety and make us feel safe and secure again. Only flawless, unspoilt, absolute adoration can become the place where our fears are overcome and our trust can rest.

When Eve listened to the voice of the devil in Eden, she found herself unsure of the response she would receive when God called her name. A shift had occurred in her perception and thinking and she falsely believed that her steadfast God had changed. Eve incorrectly believed God's reaction to her had become uncertain and unpredictable, when the truth was that God remained exactly the same. This ancient seed that God's response to us is fickle and changeable feeds our fears and our sense of insecurity. This is why it is so important that we know the truth about the nature of our God. In fact, the more we accurately recognise His breathtaking character of endless love and devotion towards us, the safer and more secure we will feel.

The God who has spent eternity devoted and committed to us is completely trustworthy. There are no actions He executes, no words He speaks and no thoughts He shares which are not saturated in His abundant love for us. For the one who chooses to believe in the works of His Son Jesus and trusts their souls to Him, there is not a single moment in time when we cannot approach Him knowing we will be welcomed with safe, compassionate, open arms. God is never angry with us because all the punishment we deserve was taken by Jesus, leaving us to revel in God's warmth and tenderness towards us. We can walk into His throne room and enjoy His company without fear of reprisal or reproach. God never changes and His desire to invest in us and believe in us never alters, no matter our attitude or actions towards Him. God's love is perfect; He is good, completely secure, absolutely constant and totally trustworthy.

The arms of God have always been open to us. His exquisite and faithful love for us has never shifted. He has been devoted to us since before the dawn of time, over and above our betrayal of Him, our hiding and our fears. His beautiful heart yearns to walk beside us every day, embracing us as our constant companion and friend, escorting us through all the high mountain top experiences of our lives, as well as the times we feel as if we are walking through the darkest valley. His faithful presence is with us from His conception of our existence to our place in eternity.

This warm blanket of safety does not lull us into a state of passivity. As a team of women, we have asked ourselves, 'What would it feel like and look like if we believed Jesus was walking right beside us?', 'How brave would we be?', 'What would we dare to attempt?'. As believers, this is not just a fabled fantasy. It is a reality. Reconnecting with our Heavenly Father brings a sense of solid assurance. It makes us courageous and we find ourselves daring to connect with others in a way we previously felt impossible and pursuing our dreams and destinies in a fashion we thought implausible. Our insecurities have strangely begun to loosen their grip on us and we have started to recognise we have an eternal rock on which our feet firmly stand.

PRAYER OF DECLARATION

You can use the following prayer, filling in the <blanks> relevant to you. Take some time to recognise and confess the lies that you have believed and replace them with the truth that the Father speaks over you.

Dear Father God,

I confess to you that I have believed the lie that
… <state the lie that you have believed>.

I ask you to forgive me for believing this lie. I realise that, by existing under its influence, I have been living an existence less than the one you created me to live.

I choose to forgive the people who have influenced this lie in my life … <state their names>.

I choose to forgive myself for believing this lie.

Father God I now make the deliberate choice to believe the truth.

I declare that … <state the truth>.

I choose to live my life firmly under the canopy of your truth, God.

Holy Spirit, I invite you now to guide me in this truth and help me to express it every day of my life.

In Jesus' name, Amen.

THE FINAL
DESTINATION

For I am convinced that
neither death nor life, neither
angels nor demons, neither
the present nor the future,
nor any powers, neither height
nor depth, nor anything else in all
creation, will be able to separate
us from the love of God that
is in Christ Jesus our Lord.

Romans 8: 38-39 (NIV)

THE RESOLVE OF EVE

As Eve ran through the dense woodland of Eden, she became vaguely aware of an unfamiliar sensation beneath the soft soles of her feet. The once soft blades of grass now seemed harsh and unforgiving, their acute edges ripping fastidiously through the smooth texture of her virgin skin, causing it to graze and bleed. The pain seemed both agonising and rewarding; a just recompense for her sinful act.

For there had been no evading the setting of the sun, and as the cool of the evening had approached, her heavenly Father had beckoned Adam and Eve to His side just as He always did. It was the tenderness and compassion in His voice which had been the most stunning surprise; the immense love in His invitation which only added to her confusion.

And so, before she knew what she was thinking, Eve found herself desperate to escape. Instead of running towards her heavenly Father as she had always done, all she wanted to do was run away from Him. In a moment of absolute despair, she crawled into a tiny, concealed clearing, small enough to hide her exhausted form. In terror and silence, she waited, holding her breath and planning her response for the moment she knew she could not avoid. She was still reeling from the words the devil had so cunningly spoken to her; still staggered by the contortion on Adam's face. Adam and Eve were convulsed with the presence of terrifying and unfamiliar emotions, a sudden sense of awareness which felt completely alien to them.

Suddenly a realisation dawned on Eve and she remembered that no amount of foliage would prevent the eyes of her God from detecting her. So, slowly she crawled from her hiding place and raised her body to full height. And with each rise in elevation, Eve made a chilling and calculated resolve. She would resist the urge to believe she could ever receive the kindness of a holy God again, she would reject the hand that was extended towards her, and she would not be held responsible for her actions. She made the choice that she would manage perfectly well without her God, she would live her life her own way, she would revel in her new-found abandonment … and she would call it freedom.

And so slowly, the light which once shone so brightly in the heart of Eve, the glow which was meant to radiate across the face of the Earth, sorrowfully grew dim; the brilliance of God's dazzling glory diminished to a mere faint reflection of all it was meant to be.

(Paraphrased from Genesis 3: 8-10)

KAREN'S STORY

I would definitely describe myself as a 'people person'. I could waste hours simply people-watching, seeing the interactions, the love and the misunderstandings! I find it fascinating to discover the unique and intricate way that people are formed and I love to find the gold in people. I love to see the potential and the gifting in people before they can even recognise it in themselves. It is so rewarding to be a part of encouraging that gifting into life. In recent times, I have come to recognise the direct link between gifting and lies, and the barrier that lies create which stops gifting being realised. The biggest discovery I made in this area was in my own life.

Some years ago, I was asked to write a parenting course with Government funding. I felt totally unqualified to do this. Surely they would find out that things didn't always go to plan in our family. I imagined that I had to be some sort of expert and I was so aware of my inadequacies. I feared that I would be exposed if I didn't get things right but, worse than that, I was scared that they would find out that I wasn't qualified for such a responsibility. Didn't they know I wasn't a psychologist, a teacher, a social worker? Whatever the perceived qualification was, I knew I didn't have it. There was no PhD after my name. I also feared what people might think. They might disagree with the material or criticise it. This further exposed my tendency to be a people-pleaser. Through that process, it exposed a huge double lie I had been believing - that I had to be perfect and I had to be qualified. The enormity of that was setting me up to fail.

Once this lie was exposed, I was able to rest in the reality that I didn't need to be perfect, I needed to be me. My family needed authenticity and the families I was working with needed permission to make mistakes. Interestingly, I never expected others to be perfect, so why would I expect the same of myself? I hadn't realised how easily I had been sucked into the disparity between believing in others and crushing myself. There was this mismatch between how I viewed what God might do, both in and through others, and how easily I dismissed myself as being unqualified. When I realised nobody wanted perfection, I was able to be real. People found this authenticity refreshing. It gave them permission to be real and honest too. This transformed the culture of the groups I was involved in and helped to form deeper relationships and stronger connections. The very thing I had hoped for actually happened when I let go of my own insecurities and exposed the lie.

I have gone on to write other courses in a number of sectors. I would like to say that I never suffer from my insecurities and that I am confident in these gifts. Yet, too often I hear that old, ugly lie whispering in my ear, telling me I'm not qualified and I'll get caught out. Being able to recognise this lie is crucial because then I can attack the lie with the truth that I am qualified by God. I realise that if God has asked me to write something, I no longer need to question whether I am qualified. I also don't need to worry about what people will think or say about me. I am doing it for Him. One of the ways that I claim victory over these lies is by surrounding myself with people who are for me and who will remind me of my identity in Christ whenever the self-doubt creeps in. What an incredible blessing to be able to encourage one another.

Chapter 32

MICHELANGELO

Every now and again in life, you read a comment that radically challenges your standing and status before almighty God. It pulls you up sharp! It makes you question and explore a presumption you previously held and dissect its content until you find its true worth. Such was my response to the following tale.

Michelangelo was an elite Italian sculptor, architect and poet of the highest order. He lived in Rome during the Renaissance period and produced some of the most exquisite and famous pieces of art the world has ever known, including the fresco of the Sistine Chapel. To call him talented and influential would be an understatement! Two of his best works were the sculptured pieces 'Pieta' and 'David', which he completed before the age of thirty. He was once asked how he created statues that so perfectly reflected the human form. He replied that 'every block of stone has a sculpture inside it' and that the task of the sculptor was simply to 'discover it'.

Michelangelo's comments deeply impacted me. It caused me to reflect on how I honestly viewed myself. Hypothetically, if I were a block of stone, what would be at the centre? When you chipped away at all the marble on the outside, who actually existed at the core and what would she be like?

Raised in abuse and abstract poverty, with a family who brawled and quarrelled every day, I had always struggled with fear and a squalid sense of worth and value. However, what really compounded my poor identity was my family's involvement in a controlling and condemning religious movement. I was programmed from a young age to believe that I was nothing more than a human child, corrupted by sin and essentially wicked. I was taught that, at the core of my being, I was filthy and it was this detestable heart of evil which resulted in my disobedient and unruly behaviour.

I am eternally grateful to God that when I reached my late teenage years I converted to Christianity and my whole world changed. Within the community of Christian believers, I learned that I was so much more than I had been lead to believe. Slowly I began to discover that I was made in the image of a beautiful God who had always loved me. I was shown the truth that, while His stunning image had been distorted by my unrighteous behaviour and that any attempt to reset the balance by doing good things for God was woefully inadequate and offensive, He had never lost sight of me, never stopped pursuing me. Most importantly, I began to recognise that it was my foolish attempt at an act of virtue, my human effort to be seen by God as pure and good, that the Bible called a 'filthy rag' and not me.

I was also grateful to learn that through the enormous sacrificial death of His son Jesus, my errant conduct was dealt with and I could be forgiven. It was at the crucifixion of Jesus that my guilt, which had been screaming at me my whole life, could at last be silenced and the peace of God could descend; that my shame, which had prevented me from believing God could ever embrace me, could be stilled and I could know God's acceptance.

It took me many years before I realised that not only did my conversion result in forgiveness, peace and acceptance, but that it altered the very core of my being - it essentially changed who I was.

Chapter 33

THE IDENTITY OF EVE

They say that the second child resembles the parent of the opposite gender. That's certainly true in my family! When you look at photographs of my oldest boy, he shows a striking similarity to his father, whereas my youngest son is the double of my own father; tall, slim, with a wide smile and a great mop of ginger hair. Both boys are gorgeous of course! And the family likenesses go deeper than mere appearances. They have the same love of the beautiful countryside and open spaces as my husband and myself while feeling quite indifferent when it comes to spending time on the beach. In the culinary department, we all love Indian food and definitely baulk at certain fast food takeaways. Over the years, they have adopted from us patterns of behaviour, family traditions and habits that they have carried on into adulthood; the good, the bad and the ugly. I have to confess, when I watch them showing warmth and hospitality, I think to myself, 'Yes, that is a Higham trait, they got that from us', but sadly other times I think, 'Ouch, that response is also a Higham trait, they must have got that one from their father!'. Only kidding, honey.

As an infant grows, they learn certain patterns of behaviour from those people around them who play a significant role in their tiny worlds. They study the face of an adult and discover that if they smile, it produces a warm, loving response. As time goes on, toddlers will hear a concerned parent say the word 'no' and, although they may resist it, venturing their little toes over the proverbial line, they learn to understand those boundaries which constitute safe and acceptable behaviour. And as the years go by, children absorb the signals given to them by adults which eventually create, among other things, the moral code a child may live by. This code may agree with or contradict their God-given sense of righteousness. During those formative years, children construct their identity, building on the principles and standards they acquire from those around them, particularly their guardians or parents. Importantly, they learn what brings worth and value and, if their lives and behaviour reflect those things, they are said to have a strong sense of 'self-worth'.

The formative years of Eve were spent in the Garden of Eden where the love and goodness of God were lavished upon her. It was within the confines of this nourishing environment that her entire identity was constructed. She was made in the image of God and all of her sense of self came from Him. Everything about Eve reflected her heavenly Father. She carried His perfection, His love, His peace, His beauty and His security. There were no disparities in Eve's identity, she really was her 'Daddy's girl'. She lived each day beneath the warmth of God's perfect love and acceptance and there she flourished without insecurities or anxiety. Eve knew exactly who she was and why she had been created.

However, when Eve ate the fruit from the tree, she went against everything that made her who she was. She might as well have taken a huge demolition ball, smashed her identity and watched as the entire structure crumbled. She had been Eve, the perfect daughter of the most High God, made in His exquisite image. She had been perfect, holy and unflawed and now she was tarnished and marred by her act of defiance. She was His creation, made to rule with Adam across the face of the Earth, and now her entire reason for existence was in jeopardy. She had never disobeyed God, in fact, she never even thought to question Him, because that was her character and now, in contrast, she had become one who had defied His wishes and broken the only rule she had ever known. Everything she had ever held to be right and true had disintegrated within her and before her. She contradicted everything she had ever known, all that she had previously stood for. The result was that, in a single immoral act, her self-image was totally disfigured, she had lost her majestic identity and her righteous sense of self-worth was left in ruins.

The Eve that had once existed was gone and the death God had once warned her about had taken place, just as He said it would.

"

'God cannot give us a happiness
and peace apart from
Himself, because it is not there.
There is no such thing.'

C. S. Lewis

Chapter 34

THE OLD MADE NEW

And so from each generation to the next, the deteriorated ruins of the broken and flawed identity of Eve have been passed on, each new life struggling to establish who they are and where their place may be in the cosmos. In fact, it could be said that we live in a world of perpetual identity crisis. Individuals, scientists and philosophers alike continuously explore the meaning of 'life's great questions', which include who we are and why we are here.

Within the ancient pages of the Bible, there are numerous descriptive verses which paint a picture of the identity and nature of a disciple of Jesus Christ. However, I believe there is none more poignant than 2 Corinthians 5: 17, because it exposes us to a substantial and life-changing truth. This verse informs us that in Christ we are now new creations, that the old has gone and the new is here. When we made the decision, through the revelation of the

Holy Spirit, to believe in the works of Jesus Christ; when we chose to turn from our old life and follow Him, Father God did something unfathomable. He recreated us and, in doing so, He changed our very nature.

The author of this verse would have intentionally and precisely selected the words and phrases he used to complete each sentence. In the Greek language, there are two words for 'new'. He might have chosen the Greek word 'neos' which means 'new in time'. We would elect to use this word today to refer to a fresh new morning or a brand new handbag, emphasising that though it may be new today, there have been expressions of the same in the past. Instead, the author preferred the word 'kainos', which interprets as 'new in nature,' implying the first of its kind, an unqualified original. At the point of our conversion, we were literally transformed. So extensive was the alteration in our nature that the Bible calls it being 'born again'.

Suddenly, we are not who we think we are. The old dilapidated building blocks of our identity have been demolished and in their place, a new tower stands majestic and beautiful. Decades of construction swept aside in a single moment. All that we had inherited from the first humans who walked the face of the Earth is irrevocably reversed and we are made new. Where once there was sin and corruption, now there is holiness and righteousness; where once there were the essential elements to produce a nature dominated by shame, now there is a being with the capacity to recognise their great worth and value;

where once we were separated from our heavenly Father, now we are secure, reconnected to our source of strength and life.

Within the text of scripture, we find the voice of God echoing through time as He calls to His people by their new name. We are His consecrated saints, sacred, holy and pure in His sight; His hallowed and devoted priesthood. His heart wells within Him as He calls us His own intimate, adopted children, selected, approved and accepted by Him. When He looks upon our faces, He sees opulent and abounding heirs to His Kingdom and His promises; royal inheritors wearing the exclusive crest of the Almighty embellished on a ring of precious metal and a robe of righteousness. Once again, the triune God casts His eyes upon His creation and He declares that it is not just good, it is very good.

Here are the thoughts of our loving God towards us and within their words of truth, there is no place for an identity of shame, a heart of unforgiveness or a mind of fear. If God has declared us worthy and laudable who are we to proclaim ourselves unfit and undeserving? It is in listening to the lies of the devil that we disqualify ourselves; it is as we embrace his voice of deceit and corruption that we become unable to receive the titles that God bestows upon us. The identity of God's creation, stolen in Eden, is restored to its rightful place.

Chapter 35

BLANKETS OF COMFORT

These magnificent thoughts of God about us are difficult for us to comprehend and even more challenging to believe. After all, we still find ourselves making mistakes, doing the wrong things, thinking unwholesome thoughts and falling into sin. We still hear the unworthy whisper of shame, guilt and fear resounding across our hearts and minds.

And yet, unfettered from our previous identity, we are emancipated to live as God always ordained. Now any disdainful thoughts, decisions or actions emanate from the lingering memories of our old selves. While at the essence of our being we are virtuous, we remain surrounded by an inconvenience that the Bible calls the flesh. The flesh is a like a shadowy blanket under which we are often invited to crawl. We are allured there by the lies of the devil and the security of familiarity. But it is a false and dangerous haven because the edges of the blanket quickly become snared and weighed down. Before we know it, we are trapped beneath its power, struggling to shift or escape. We are told in Scripture to 'throw off' the ways of the flesh, to resist the enticements of the devil's lies and withstand the lure of the previous ways of life.

You see, when the devil devised his despicable plan to decimate God's beautiful creation, he intended to pursue its completion to his last breath. He has not given up the fight even though God had devised a battle plan to bring victory long before the devil had even begun to conceive the temptation of Eve. Using the fingerprints of our old life, our habitual patterns of thinking and doing, he stalks us and tempts us back to the ways of our abandoned self. He screams the timeworn lies of our imperfection and worthlessness in our ear and we are channelled back into our now outdated, protective and defensive responses. He tells us that we are alone and unsafe and we hunker down beneath our aprons of concealment, forgetting all we were meant to be.

It is at this point that we stray. We find ourselves acting in a manner which fails to reflect our new God-given nature. The devil is delighted by our vulnerability and pushes on further with his attack. He informs us that God is not trustworthy, that His work of redemption is shallow and ineffective and we cannot expect God to forgive us yet again. But we are not the fearful, timid people we once were. And so we hold our arm out in front of us, we extend our hand vertically as if to form an impenetrable wall and boldly we declare, 'Enough is enough!'. We demolish his sacrilege with the truth that his words are blatant lies and that God's eternal love has already redeemed us, that the death of Jesus was sufficient and that our confession will always bring God's forgiveness because we belong to Him.

What is more, our gracious God will take our failures, the very thing the devil would use to harm and dishearten us and He will spin them around for our good. Though there may be consequences to our actions, just as there was for Eve, God will not abandon us. He will take every negative circumstance in our lives and He will show us the glory of His goodness through them. In our weakness He will reveal His strength, in our loneliness He will surround us by His loving arms and in our failure He will expound His immense faithfulness and commitment to us. And as we see His goodness and receive His kindness, we shift a little further towards Him and we feel a little safer with Him. And as we trust Him, our guard begins to lower and our true colours shine through.

In this sense, we are holy but our perfection is not yet complete. In this way, although at the point of our conversion we were made new, we journey daily towards a life fully aligned with the person God always intended us to be. Sanctification is a process, but for the believer who has accepted Christ, it emanates not from a place of wickedness and despair, but from a core of wholeness and salvation. We walk from a renewed identity, not a decimated self and we progress from glory into further glory.

Chapter 36

RECOGNISING
HIS PRESENCE

There are moments in my life when I have been on the receiving end of unmerited and unwarranted generosity. I remember some years ago when my husband had been ill and unable to work. As a consequence, there were no funds for our annual, summertime family holiday, an event I always looked forward to. In her kindness, a lady whom we hardly knew invited myself and my family to use her beautiful holiday cottage in Wiltshire. She simply handed us the keys and a piece of paper with an address on it and allowed us to choose the preferred date for our family get-away. When we arrived, I was astonished because the cottage was fitted with very expensive, luxurious furnishings and fragile antiques. Bearing in mind that she knew we had two active, adventurous boys, I was amazed that she had trusted us so willingly. She had freely allowed us to stay there, even though there was no guarantee that items would not get damaged or broken. From my perspective, it was an enormous act of trust and kindness, a really lavish gift.

Our God is unbelievably generous and as such, He heaps thoughtful gifts upon us all the time, even when we do not recognise it. God has a benevolent nature and He cannot act in any way other than to be true to Himself. He does not leave us to battle the lies of the devil and succumb to the prevailing power of his influence alone. The Bible tells us that within every Christian believer the Spirit of the resurrected Christ dwells. Along with the presence of God and Jesus, a new believer's identity is shifted as the indwelling of the Holy Spirit takes place. It is astonishing that God would trust us with such a precious and valued part of Himself.

The Holy Spirit is a stunning and integral part of the triune Godhead. He was there at the very beginning when the world, the Garden of Eden and the first humans were created. We were made to reflect as much His nature as any other person of Elohim, the ancient name for God in His fullness.

It is the Holy Spirt who plays a vital role in our conversion, convincing us of God's judgement and our need for salvation. He opens the heart of unbelievers to receive truth and then He guides us in it. He prompts us and reminds us of that which is wholesome and honest. He brings back to memory certainty about who we are, who our God is, and reminds us of His immense and passionate love for us. The Holy Spirit comforts us when we are sorrowful and helps us to draw near to our Father where we can rest in peace and contentment. Essentially, He causes us to radiate the reflection of the Father that we were created to reveal; the fruit of the Spirit displaying the attributes of the Almighties in all their splender and glory.

When the devil lied to Eve, he robbed her of her identity. He stole from her the very essence of who she was and he left her unique and stunning God-given nature in tatters. But he foolishly underestimated God's desire for His beautiful handiwork. He had no notion that God would go so far and be so fanatical in His pursuit of His own. In the death of Jesus, the avid passion of God for His children is revealed and in the life of the Holy Spirit, God's steadfast devotion and dedication to humanity is exposed. He has made a way for His spectacular creation to reclaim their identity, an inheritance afforded to them before the fabric of the universe was formed. He has also placed within the framework of each believer the astonishing ability to walk a life of natural existence while reflecting the supernatural nature of the glorious Godhead.

A destiny as old as Eden prepared for us since the dawn of time.

"

'Courage is contagious.
When a brave man takes
a stand, the spines of others
are often stiffened.'

Billy Graham

KIM'S STORY

I have been a Christian for twenty-five years and, in all that time, I have struggled with speaking about Jesus and my faith. I have always been a quiet person and, as a teenager, painfully shy so really it's no surprise that I didn't like speaking out. However, over the years God began to gradually release me to be the person He created me to be, but my freedom to speak of Jesus didn't really change.

When asked by anyone when I had become a Christian, my answer would be 1991. However, God reminded me one day that actually something happened years before that. As a child of eleven or twelve years-old, I had asked Jesus into my heart during a Christian holiday club. I had returned home with a book all about Jesus, maybe similar to 'Why Jesus?'. This book was placed in a drawer beside my bed and my Mum encouraged me to keep it there because my Dad wouldn't want to talk about it. He was rather discouraging about faith issues, and I certainly didn't want to make him cross or angry. My fleeting encounter with Jesus was snuffed out and no relationship or understanding grew. I really didn't think about this commitment anymore or even why I wasn't encouraged to speak about Jesus.

When I finally came back to know Jesus as my Father in 1991, the tight bud of a rose gradually began to open into a full-bloomed rose, as His Holy Spirit worked in me. The shy person who believed people weren't interested in what she had to say was gradually being healed, and small changes were happening. My greatest fear was of speaking in front of groups of people; becoming very flustered, blushed and embarrassed. Slowly this changed and my confidence grew, knowing the Holy Spirit was at work in me and my Father was encouraging me along the way.

Later, I heard teaching into the lies I have believed and began to understand how they distorted my thinking. God reminded me of my little book beside the bed and how I had been silenced about my faith. I had believed all those years that I wasn't to speak about Jesus because I would upset people or make them cross and angry! My heavenly Father wanted that to change and He was going to release me to have a voice people would listen to. I had to renounce the lies that speaking about Jesus would upset people, and replace them with the truth; that my Father God loved me dearly and I would never make Him cross or angry. I was the apple of His eye!

Many years ago, I had received a prophetic word about 'coming out from under the table because I had been hidden for long enough'. I really felt this word was so true and never more so than when Jesus was bringing me out of hiding. The truth, that I had hidden for so long in my drawer beside my bed, was that I loved Jesus then and so much more now! No more to be frightened or scared of what people thought of my Jesus or the words I spoke of Him. My voice was to be released to speak truth and freedom to others, so they too may know and experience the Father's love for themselves.

... being confident of this, that
He who began a good work in you
will carry it on to completion
until the day of Christ Jesus.

Philippians 1: 6 (NIV)

Chapter 37

THE DECISION
OF FAITH

The gift of God's stunning love and His eternal destiny for each of our lives sits enticingly on the hallway table, ready for us to embrace it. And like all gifts that are given to us by God, they are accessed by grace on His part and faith on ours. In this case, it is the faith to believe that the words and works of God are true and hold precious and treasured eternal consequences for us. And that the words and works of the devil are false and will lead us to a place of ultimate damnation. The conscious and life-changing decision to have faith in the death of Jesus is applicable and relevant to us, both as a corporate humanity and an individual soul. Just as we choose to renounce the lie that we are not worthy to enter the presence of a holy God, so we accept the truth that the work of Christ was sufficient to make it happen.

It is easy to get caught up in the lie that the Christian life is all about what we do; that ultimately it is our actions that are the currency which determines how effective and dedicated we are as followers of Christ. But it is not. There are numerous verses within the Bible that teach us that it is not the surface actions of our behaviour which are essential, rather the attitudes and motivations behind them. Our actions are simply extensions of our belief, the outward working of the thoughts we hold; a presentation of what exists deep within our souls. In the secret world of our subconscious, our beliefs come unquestionably into play. It is from this shrouded place that all else is expressed; our motivations, attitudes and actions. That is why our beliefs are so important, they simply influence everything.

Faith and belief are utterly interconnected. Having faith that God had every intention of completely nullifying all the damage to humanity that was inflicted in Eden is to believe that God's desire is to be with us, that He yearns for us to be in a loving and wholesome relationship with Him. It is to believe that His longing heart only ever desires connection between us, never separation. It is to believe that He has made a way to restore His treasured creation back to their God-reflecting beauty. Having faith in the steps that God has signposted for us in the Bible is to believe that God only has good for us, that He is not out for revenge or to do us harm, but He has and has always had our best interests at heart. It is to declare that He is essentially good and can therefore only do us good. Having faith that we are forgiven every single time we fail is to believe that the work of God's son at Calvary actually achieved what God intended it to and therefore we dare not deny it. It is to believe that every one of us who has lived in guilt, shame and fear has been redeemed. Having faith that God will provide our needs is to believe that He is intrinsically all powerful and can influence every situation, regardless of how hopeless it may appear. Having faith that we are significant in the sight of God, that our time here on Earth holds purpose and meaning, is to believe that we were created for the purpose of reflecting the glory of a dazzling beautiful God.

Belief is the foundation of faith, while faith is the ultimate state of confidence in that belief.

In the Book of Hebrews, we read that faith is the belief that God exists and that He is a rewarder of those who seek Him. This is the fundamental and definitive request of God to His precious children. That we crush forever the lie that the devil whispered to Eve that God is suspiciously untrustworthy, and that we choose to have faith again in His richest goodness and unfathomable love. It is from this point that the freedoms of the Christian faith become endless. It is from this point that we can truly be restored to all God created us to be.

Therefore, there is now no condemnation for those who are in Christ Jesus, because through Christ Jesus the law of the Spirit who gives life has set you free from the law of sin and death. For what the law was powerless to do because it was weakened by the flesh,

God did by sending His own Son in the likeness of sinful flesh to be a sin offering. And so He condemned sin in the flesh, in order that the righteous requirement of the law might be fully met in us, who do not live according to the flesh but according to the Spirit.

Romans 8: 1-4 (NIV)

Chapter 38

THE JOURNEY SO FAR

When I look back across my years as a Christian believer, I am amazed at how much I have actually changed and how far the love of God has carried me. So much of my behaviour was once rooted in fear, guilt and shame. So many of my actions born out of the lies I had foolishly listened to; falsehoods I had believed about God, others and myself that I had far too easily embraced. I would love to say that I no longer concede to the devil's lies, but the truth is that he is a relentless adversary who persists daily in his assaults. But every time I recognise that I have been behaving in a manner which reflects fear or worthlessness, I can at least sit down and try and examine where the root of my insecurity or despair comes from. Have I been believing a lie? What do I believe about God, others and myself that has motivated me to think and act in a way which does not reflect the nature, goodness and glory of God? It's a really good question to ask myself. It's a really good question to ask yourself too.

Over the years I have come to realise that the steps of freedom are available for me to walk in. I just need to clear the space for my mind to explore the route and allow the Holy Spirit to guide me. Within the pages of God's precious Word, His voice speaks clearly. He points me to the act of confession, authenticity and humility which reveals my need for the intervention of a redeeming God and removes the barriers which I chose to erect. These steps alter my thinking and renew my mind. They manoeuvre me away from believing the falsehoods of the devil and into the path of the truths of a faithful God. They direct me towards the choice of faith and trust which allows me to rest safely in the arms of the God who simply adores me.

Furthermore, these steps pull me further into the various pockets of the community of humanity to which I belong, my family, my friends and those I connect with every day. As I dare to be more open, I find my relationships strengthened and my friendships deepen. Hence the image of the triune God is reflected as the love between us grows stronger and shines more brilliantly.

Equally, I find I am more at peace with myself. I understand now why I act the way I do, why I doubt and know fear. It all comes back to Eden, to the place where it all began. It all comes back to the very beginning. But more importantly, I am learning to really believe that the death of Jesus made a way for everything to change. My guilt can be quietened by Christ's sacrifice because I am proclaimed innocent, the grip of shame is loosened because I recognise that my identity is no longer wretched and my fears can be stilled by the comfort of God's presence. When I choose to believe the words of God over the words of the devil, then there is a daily transformation which leads me further on to the place of being able to reflect the beauty of God, the treasure within which I gratefully carry. I am learning to walk daily towards this existence, the purpose for which I was lovingly created, the ultimate expression of my God-given destiny.

The thief comes only to steal
and kill and destroy; I have
come that they may have life,
and have it to the full.

John 10: 10 (NIV)

Chapter 39

IN THE END

I once watched a very famous missionary on a conference platform in the USA. She was so full of enthusiasm and passion that it bordered on crazy! Watching her dance around the stage, laughing and crying out to God for her precious Mozambique left you exhausted, exhilarated and inspired all at the same time. I have to tell you I was impressed and just a little envious. How does anyone get that level of hunger and conviction about the call of God on their lives? How does anyone believe that much? But what I was really saying was why don't I carry that much passion in my own life? Why don't I believe that much? And if it's out there, how do I get a piece? I left the conference with my head spinning and my mind preoccupied with my recently acquired questions.

A few weeks after the event, I decided to go on a personal retreat. And by that, I mean I borrowed a friend's empty house for five days and spent the whole time praying, soaking in worship, meditating on specific scriptures and reading a couple of my favourite authors for inspiration. It was a great time. While I was there, I decided to ask God about the conference I had just attended. Expectantly, I asked Him, 'How do you get that much love and passion in your life, God?', 'How do I get that much love and passion in 'my' life?'. Eventually, the answer came but it wasn't what I expected. I felt God say, 'Shirley, you are asking the wrong question. It's not about the amount of love you have for me; it's about the amount of love I have for you. It's not about the amount of passion you have for me; it's about the amount of passion I have for you.' I was overwhelmed and humbled. So often in my life, I have thought that my Christian walk is dependent on my thoughts and actions for God when really it's all about Him and His never ending commitment and desire that He holds for us.

The truth is, it's always been about Him. The onslaught that was Eden was never really aimed at humanity anyway, rather it was the devil's assault of envy and jealousy against a beautiful and almighty God. The devil could never have destroyed God so he decided to disfigure His creation, violating us with lies and influences that he knew would catastrophically mutilate the perfect reflection of God they were created to display.

And so we find ourselves with a choice. Do we cooperate in the strategy of the devil, listening as Eve did to his twisted lies? Do we cocoon ourselves in a protective layer and remain hidden, succumbing to the shame and fear that is perpetuated from the lies that we so naively believe?

Or do we allow ourselves to be convinced that the restoring work of Jesus was sufficient to redeem us, walking away from the shadow of condemnation and resting in the arms of forgiveness? To put it simply, are we ready to have faith in the voice of our God over and above the voice of the devil?

Let us remember that we are redeemed and changed through the death of Jesus, but God did not perform such an act of outlandish mercy simply to pay our debt and deliver us from our sin, per se. It was not our redemption that was the ultimate definitive outcome, rather the prize set before Him was the reconciliation of His beloved creation to Himself. His heart was to address the reason for our fear, shame and separation, to deal once and for all with any excuses we may ever carry for turning our faces from Him and rejecting His love. His commitment to us remains eternally unshakeable and ceaselessly unwavering.

And so God implores us to dare to decide that in every second of our lives, from this day forward, we will believe in God's voice above all others, perceiving ourselves and this world through the eyes of our loving and accepting heavenly Father. To do so is to walk daily in Christian faith and belief; this mandatory step an essential action in escaping the doubts and fears that can infiltrate our lives and dominate our existence.

Our loving God is waiting. His attention is fixed upon us as we make our daily choices. With soft piercing eyes and a gentle compelling voice, He beckons us along this journey, knowing that ultimately it will lead His beloved children home. He calls us again to be people who love our God and each other as we were created to love, to submissively rest in the strong arms of our tender God and to walk through life as we were eternally destined. God's pathway to return to all He created us to be is laid. It was prepared before the foundation of the Earth, ready for our fragile and tentative feet to tread.

"We all have unique gifts waiting to be discovered. For me, writing a book has been an adventure, one that has been made easier by people who have supported me on the journey. Simplicate have provided that support and made the experience more enjoyable. I urge you to pursue your dreams, express the creativity God has given you, and join with others, like I have, to help make that a reality."

Shirley Higham

---

simplicate

WRITING A BOOK?

LOOKING TO SELF-PUBLISH?

At *Simplicate*, we work with new and existing authors to bring their books to life. A digital agency with a difference, we have a range of flexible options for authors. We can help you to navigate the myriad challenges in publishing books, courses, resources or training, and come alongside you to walk the journey with you, as you realise the full potential of your next project. Get in touch today.

Email: *info@simplicate.org*

Website: *www.simplicate.org*

"There is something about worship music that feeds the soul like nothing else. I find music to be a fantastic medium for getting God's truths to sit in my heart, as well as my head. There are certain albums that bless me and capture God's heart for his children. *Home Is Here* by *Crowned* is one such album, perfectly summing up in music the essence of *The Little Book of Eve*."   *Shirley Higham*

God has personally and permanently adopted each of us. He is a good Father. Everything He does in our direction is because of His love for us. *Home Is Here* is the first worship album by *Crowned*, a collective of songwriters, singers and musicians from across Dorset, UK.

Available via all digital stores, or via the
Crowned website: *www.crowned.org.uk*

ABOUT THE AUTHOR

Shirley Higham has been involved in ministering to women for well over a decade. Nothing brings her more pleasure than watching women begin to recognise their worth before God and then to go on to live their lives as He always intended. Over the years, she has juggled being a leader in her local church with working as a nurse and being a mum to two gorgeous boys. Recently she has discovered that, along with preaching, hiking and chocolate, she also has a love of blogging and writing. She has a BA in Applied Theology and believes passionately in the power of the Word of God to bring about beauty and transformation.

Visit Shirley's website for more information

TRUTH AND FAVOUR

www.truthandfavour.com